ISSUES
IN
CANADIAN
HISTORY

Imperialism and Nationalism, 1884-1914: A Conflict in Canadian Thought

Edited by
CARL BERGER

THE COPP CLARK PUBLISHING COMPANY
TORONTO

[1794]

ISBN 0.7730.3108.1

© 1969 The Copp Clark Publishing Company

Contents

Introduction

Imperialism in Canada presented many faces and its story has been told from various perspectives. Its aim was to consolidate the British Empire through military, economic and constitutional devices. Those Canadians who supported imperial unity, or imperial federation, believed that Canada could attain national status only by maintaining the connection with the Empire and by acquiring an influence within its councils. Their opponents were convinced that imperialism was incompatible with Canada's national interests, internal unity, and self-government. The conflict between these two forces was a major theme in Canadian life in the thirty years before the First World War, and the struggle was bitter and divisive. It was fought out in many arenas, in Parliament, at Colonial and Imperial Conferences and in polemical literature, and it centered upon several issues—commercial policy, participation in the Boer War, and military and naval preparedness. But it was above all fought out in the minds of Canadians, and it is from this point of view, as a problem in Canadian intellectual history, that it is presented in this book. The questions raised here do not concern, at least not primarily, elections, the formulation of tariff policy or the problems of military co-operation. These readings are intended rather to bring into sharper focus the guiding ideas and divergent conceptions of the Canadian future that underlay the clash between imperialism and nationalism.

Imperialism and nationalism are vague words which must be defined in terms of their historical context. The organized movement for imperial unity originated in the later 1880's. The cumulative impact of the long depression, the failure of Macdonald's National Policy to generate prosperity and economic integration, and the cultural crisis that followed the execution of Louis Riel, produced a widespread feeling of pessimism about Canada's future. The commitment of

1

the Liberal party to unrestricted reciprocity, or free trade with the United States, climaxed the fears of those who, rightly or wrongly, identified such a policy with continentalism. It was at this point—in 1887 and 1888—that branches of the Imperial Federation League, an organization founded in England in 1884, were set up in Canada, and they quickly became the centres of a perfervid British Canadian patriotism. As a countermeasure to reciprocity, the supporters of imperial unity advocated the idea of an economic union of the Empire to be secured through preferential tariffs. Imperial preference remained the central plank in the agenda of Canadian imperialism long after unrestricted reciprocity was defeated in the election of 1891, and long after the Liberal party rejected it in 1893. Canadian imperialists were far more emphatic on the commercial aspects of imperial unity than were their counterparts in England. In fact the difference of opinion between those who stressed imperial preference and those who placed their faith in military and naval co-operation was one of the chief reasons why the Imperial Federation League disintegrated in 1893. Its branches in Canada, however, were simply reconstituted as organs of the British Empire League. When in 1897 the new Liberal government of Wilfrid Laurier extended a preference on British manufactured commodities entering Canada, the action was widely hailed as a practical implementation of the imperial ideal.

Imperial unity was as much a state of mind as a political platform, and the appeals of those who underlined the necessity for Canada to maintain and strengthen the British connection customarily transcended commercial and economic arguments. The leading spokesmen of imperial unity—Colonel George T. Denison of Toronto, a police magistrate and military thinker, George R. Parkin, a New Brunswick born

teacher and writer, and Rev. George M. Grant, Principal of Queen's University—all believed that Canada could only grow and survive if it held fast to the imperial connection. They were convinced, or they convinced themselves, partly through their reading of Goldwin Smith's plea for continental union, *Canada and the Canadian Question* (1891), that though unrestricted reciprocity might bring prosperity it would also ultimately end in political extinction. As a consequence, their arguments against a particular trade policy moved away from a discussion of the comparative prices of eggs in Toronto and Pittsburg to an attempt to awaken an appreciation for, and an attachment to, those traditions and institutions which in their minds made the Canadian nationality worthy of preservation. In this sense imperial unity began as a defence of Canada.

In the later eighties and early nineties imperial unity found its main support in the older section of English Canada and particularly among the descendants of the United Empire Loyalists. Both Denison and Parkin traced their roots back to the Loyalists who were described, in the mythology of the day, as "Canada's Pilgrim Fathers." Though the Imperial Federation League in 1889 counted one quarter of the members of the Dominion Parliament in its ranks, its most vocal and devoted supporters were drawn from a narrow group of politicians, lawyers, teachers, and Protestant ministers. It received no support from labour or the farming population, and in French Canada its progress was viewed firstly with indifference, then alarm, and finally with massive hostility. This is hardly surprising. Members of the Orange Order, who interpreted imperial federation to mean Protestant supremacy, were often members of the League, and D'Alton McCarthy, the leader of the Equal Rights Movement which endeavoured to limit

French language rights and separate schools to Quebec alone, was prominent among the adherents of imperialism. Not all imperialists, of course, were supporters of Orangeism and Equal Rights. One of the most sympathetic defences of the state-supported separate schools of Manitoba was penned by G. M. Grant, who had been instrumental in deposing McCarthy from his position in the League because he had jeopardized the cause of imperial unity. Yet in general, the obvious racial overtones of the imperial sentiment, and the strange allies with whom the imperialist consorted, were enough to alienate French Canada.

Born in a period of doubt and despair, imperialism by the late 1890's had become more impatient, assertive and bellicose. The appointment of Joseph Chamberlain to the Colonial Office in 1895 signalized the increasing seriousness of purpose of British imperialism. In 1899, in spite of his own personal predisposition to remain uninvolved, Laurier was forced by public pressure in English Canada to dispatch Canadian soldiers to fight in the Boer War. This action was in itself a testimony to the growing strength of the imperial cause. Fourteen years before, Macdonald had shrugged off similar suggestions that Canada aid Britain in the Soudan and his reaction was endorsed by Denison, one of the most militant of Canadian imperialists who was never one to miss a war if he could help it. The Boer War was the decisive event in the history of Canadian imperialism. To many English Canadians it was not a matter of aiding England. For them that experience was invested with all the enthusiasm of nationalism. Canada's participation, niggardly though some thought it was, marked the entry of the Dominion into world politics. She had become a force within the Empire and her path forward was straight and clear. Now that Canadians had demonstrated their willingness to support the Empire with more than emotional speeches, was it not only fair that they be accorded some influence over the direction of imperial foreign policy? French Canadians saw the matter very differently. The spectacle of Canadians fighting in so remote a war, one waged against a non-British minority with which they so easily identified themselves, generated an imperialist reaction which grew and gained momentum. Some time before, the nationalist Premier of Quebec, Honoré Mercier, had warned that the imperial federationists wanted "us to assume, in spite of ourselves, the responsibilities and dangers of a sovereign state which will not be ours. They seek to expose us to vicissitudes of peace and war . . . ; to wrest from our arms our sons, . . . and send them off to bloody and distant wars, which we shall not be able to stop or prevent."[1] And the prophecy had come true. In 1899 Henri Bourassa left the Liberal Party charging that Laurier had capitulated to pressure from the Colonial Office and had thereby established a precedent, fatal to Canadian self-government, that Canada must fight in all imperial wars. In 1903, in conjunction with a group of young French Canadian nationalists, Bourassa founded the Ligue Nationaliste to combat the imperial menace. The zest with which imperialists had supported the South African war was proof to them of the essentially colonial-minded character of English Canada.

These two extremes, the one demanding that Canada take up imperial obligations and be accorded a voice in Empire affairs, the other insisting on Canadian neutrality and freedom from such burdens, were not easily reconciled, and for some time Laurier did not try to reconcile them. He turned aside Chamberlain's suggestions at the Colonial Conference of 1902 that co-operation be institutionalized. Though he declared in the same year that Canada must take

some steps to ensure her security, and though in 1903, after the unpopular Alaska Boundary decision, he also urged that the Dominion make her own foreign policy, Laurier made no fundamental decisions in either direction, except for taking over the management of the naval bases at Halifax and Esquimalt. The imperial question lay quiescent until the "naval scare" of 1909 made postponement impossible. The threat that the German ship-building programme would undermine the supremacy of British sea-power set off a wide-ranging and acrimonious debate over what stand Canada should take. The imperialists contended that Canada, now strong and prosperous, should help sustain the force upon which her own security depended; to the anti-imperialists this appeared as the payment of tribute to the motherland whose interests were very different from Canada's. In reality the debate was more complex than this, for even imperialists were in disagreement about the exact extent and nature of Canada's contribution to imperial defence. But Laurier's proposal for the creation of a Canadian navy which in times of crisis would become part of the British fleet angered both extremes and in part accounted for his defeat in 1911. Long before this time Bourassa had come to think of Laurier as the main instrument of the imperialist conspiracy. On July 13, 1911 he wrote in Le Devoir: "English and African soldiers fell on the veldt for the glory of Chamberlain; women and children died of shame and misery for the grandeur of Laurier; children's entrails were cut out in the Concentration camps for the honour of the Empire." From the imperialist Stephen Leacock, on the other hand, came this greeting at the news of Laurier's defeat:

Sir Wilfrid, it may be said, with all the gentleness of speech which is becoming in speaking of such a man on such an occasion, touched in this election

upon the one point on which he never fully enjoyed the confidence of the Canadian people — our relations to the British Empire. It has been his fortunate lot to represent us on great occasions. He has ridden for us in coaches of State, to the plaudits of a London multitude. He has coined phrases for us, of summoning us to Imperial councils and the like, grandiloquent in the utterance, but meaning less and less as they recede into retrospect. That he never really understood the feelings of his English-speaking fellow citizens of Canada towards their Mother Country, that he never really designed to advance the cause of permanent Imperial unity — these things may well be doubted . . . We are . . . groping for something which we desire but still seek in vain. The great problem of our common future is to find an organic basis of lasting union. [2]

Such was the burden of the two extremes which tore apart the man who searched for the fragile consensus.

In the thirty years before 1914, the difference between nationalism and imperialism was much more complicated than the desire for Canadian autonomy on the one hand and a willingness to live under Downing Street rule on the other. Not even the anti-imperialists thought it was that simple. John Ewart, for example who defined nationalism as the end of subordination of one state to another, remarked that those Canadian imperialists with whom he was acquainted were really Canadian nationalists. And within the terms of his own definition he was right. What divided those who called themselves nationalists from those who preferred to be known as imperialists was not the question of whether Canada should manage her own affairs and have the power to formulate a foreign policy expressive of her interests; what divided them was disagreement over how these powers were to be acquired and for what purposes they were to be employed. The imperialists saw the British Empire as the vehicle in which Canada would attain national status; the anti-

imperialists were so convinced of the incompatability of imperial and Canadian interests that they saw all schemes for co-operation as reactionary and anti-national. In a fundamental sense, therefore, the differences between, say, Stephen Leacock and Henri Bourassa stemmed from their very different ideas about Canada, her history, and place in the world. The only way to understand the conflict between the positions these two men embodied is to understand the divergent conceptions which underlay them.

There are some limitations to the purpose of this volume as well as some particular problems that are raised by such an approach. It is not intended as a self-contained presentation of every facet and ramification of the nationalist-imperialist conflict. Such a project would require several more volumes. Nor does the approach suggest that intellectual history offers some magical key that will unlock all the puzzles and problems raised by the theme. And certainly it is not intended to supersede all other approaches. Someone has said that the practice of intellectual history is like trying to nail jelly to the wall, and indeed the entities that are subject to examination are nebulous and intangible. Any exact and scientific way of measuring the force and impact of ideas, furthermore, has yet to be devised, and the question must always arise as to the connection between ideas and the motives of those active men of power who made the crucial decisions. Yet when all this is said our understanding of Canadian history would be narrow indeed if we left out of account the climate of opinion in which the battle between imperialism and anti-imperialism took place. In the accounts of the Boer War crisis or the naval debate, for example, one invariably encounters allusions to the "imperialist pressure from English Canada" for this or that policy; yet one often comes away with the impression that we are told a good deal more about how extreme positions were accommodated or compromised at the centre than we learn about the extremes themselves. If we want to understand what imperialism and nationalism meant we must look to those who were the exponents and interpreters of these beliefs and try to grasp what these convictions meant to them. Only by doing so can we appreciate why their opposition was so fundamental and why Canadian historians are still divided as to the meaning of imperialism as a factor in Canadian history.

The selections from the historians in Part Three have been chosen with certain criteria in mind. The secondary literature on imperialism and imperial relations in Canada is vast in bulk and for the most part is devoted to investigations of tariff policy, specific crises like the Boer War, or, more generally, the impact of imperial problems in politics. Since the focus of this volume is on the ideas of nationalism and imperialism, few of these works, some of them very excellent studies, were directly and immediately appropriate. Because of this fact, and also because of the lack of scholarly studies in intellectual history, the selections presented here are therefore intended to illustrate the different ways in which historians have looked at the imperial-nationalist theme in a general and reflective way. They are also meant to suggest what happened to these ideas in the long run and how historians, looking back over a couple of generations, have weighed their significance.

1. Quoted in George R. Parkin, *Imperial Federation The Problem of National Unity* (London, 1892), pp. 85-6.
2. Stephen Leacock, *The Great Victory in Canada*, (reprint from *The National Review*, London, 1911), p. 12.

Clash of Opinion

Whoever wishes to know what Canada is, and to understand the Canadian question, should begin by turning from the political to the natural map. . . . Whether the four blocks of territory constituting the Dominion can for ever be kept by political agencies united among themselves and separate from their Continent, of which geographically, economically, and with the exception of Quebec ethnologically, they are parts, is the Canadian question.

GOLDWIN SMITH

Dr. Goldwin Smith once said that "few have fought against geography and prevailed." Man triumphs continually over geography or nature in any form. . . . Would it not be more to the purpose to ask, how few have fought against human nature, especially against its best elements, and prevailed?

GEORGE M. GRANT

In the United States, . . . the principle of "manifest destiny" . . . runs like a thread through every page of its international history. . . . Most Canadians believe today that the United States has shown a steady, deliberate dislike of their country and has pursued a policy more or less injurious to their interests.

J. CASTELL HOPKINS

Of the antipathy to Americans sedulously kept up within select circles and in certain interests, there is absolutely none among the Canadian people at large. It would be strange if there were any, considering that half of them have brothers, sons, or cousins on the American side of the Line.

GOLDWIN SMITH

Is there any reason why an Imperialist should not be a Canadian nationalist? I am firmly persuaded that there is no such reason.

JOHN EWART

Imperialism means . . . the realization of a Greater Canada . . . I . . . am an Imperialist because I will not be a Colonial.

STEPHEN LEACOCK

The controlling idea of the French Canadian is to retain his language, religion and civil institutions. . . . In the Great Republic the French Canadian would run the risk of being blotted out as was the Frenchman of Louisiana. In an independent Canada he would hold his own with difficulty. He must in the long run vote to follow the Empire in whatsoever direction its development may lead.

GEORGE PARKIN

For a long time annexation to the United States was most abhorrent to the French-Canadian. . . . But should . . . Canadian autonomy [be] encroached upon in any way, should he be hurried into any Im-

6

perial scheme and forced to assume fresh obligations, he would prefer throwing in his lot with his powerful neighbour to the South.

HENRI BOURASSA

The Monroe Doctrine must be taken as a fact, not as a theory. It is no more unbecoming in us to trust to its protection than for any of the smaller powers of Europe, like Belgium, Holland, Bulgaria and Switzerland, to shield themselves behind the conflicting interests of their big neighbors.

OLIVAR ASSELIN

There is widely spread in Canada a vague feeling that if anything turns up we shall be protected by a curious combination of the Monroe Doctrine and the British navy. I object . . . to the word protection. When I lived in England, one heard of a certain type of ladies who lived in some parts of London under the protection of certain gentlemen. Theirs was a profession considered to be more lucrative than honourable, and I have no desire that this country of mine should be either the kept woman of the United States, or the harlot of the Empire.

WILLIAM L. GRANT

To the Christian, the moralist, the philanthropist, no inspiration could be greater than that which might well spring from observing the growing strength of the Empire, and from reflection that this immense energy might be turned in directions which would make for the world's good.

GEORGE PARKIN

To sum up the theory [of Imperialism], the colonies are to purchase, by paying the tax of blood, the advantages of a preferential treatment in the British market for their farm produce.

HENRI BOURASSA

. . . the ideal of becoming the granary of the Empire is constantly held up to Canada. . . . Doubtless, for all time, the world will cherish the glorious legacy of Athens; but what idea of Athenian greatness had those bucolic barbarians from the north who supplied the city with grain?

ADAM SHORTT

. . . the British Empire is our Empire, as it is the Empire of every part; and we are as much interested in the safety of the heart of it as in any portion, and we have the right to urge that England shall take steps to make her condition safe.

GEORGE T. DENISON

For the colonies the alternative [to imperial federation] is independence, when, as small and struggling nationalities, they will have to take their place in a world which has developed distinct tendencies towards the agglomeration of immense states, and where absorption or comparative insignificance can alone await them. For Great Britain the choice is between amalgamating permanently in some way her strength and resources with those of the colonies, or abdicating the relatively foremost place which she now holds among the nations.

GEORGE PARKIN

A rough balance of power within the English-speaking world seemed essential to him [Macdonald] to ensure Canada's survival. The diplomatic and military support of Great Britain could alone offset the political preponderance of the United States. . . . The first half of the twentieth century witnessed a persistent

decline in the power of Great Britain. It saw an even more impressive and steady rise in the . . . authority of the United States.

DONALD CREIGHTON

Essentially the conflict between Ewart and those who believed in the consolidation of the British Empire revolved around the interpretation of the objective-nationalism.

DAVID FARR

As one looks back now, it seems evident that the North American isolationists, English-Canadian and French-Canadian, were blind in their failure to see the realities of the international balance of power in this twentieth century.

FRANK UNDERHILL

Imperial unity, however described, was a matter of national survival for Canadians; . . . Canadian supporters of imperial unity were ardent Canadian nationalists, who had no intention of bartering away hard-won rights of responsible Government. . . . The desired end was the strengthening of Canada, not aid to Britain, but the better to defend the Dominion against the United States.

NORMAN PENLINGTON

It was really a spirit of nationalism that was stirring, but for a time it took the channel of imperialism. Imperial partnership might be a permanent ideal, or it might be only a step toward nationhood, but in any case it represented a distinct advance over colonialism.

O. D. SKELTON

Part I

The Imperialist Argument

Just as the imperial movement in the late 1880's was a reaction to the disappointments of the period and the challenge of continentalism, the imperialist ideology was very much a response to a single book which summed up the weaknesses of Canada and prescribed her dissolution. Goldwin Smith's *Canada and the Canadian Question* (1891) is unquestionably one of the most cogent critiques of Canada ever written and it remains the classic statement of North American continentalism. An English liberal of the Manchester school, Smith had taught history at Oxford and Cornell Universities and had settled in Toronto in 1871. There he devoted his efforts to creating an independent journalism, encouraging Canadian intellectual life, and commenting on the Canadian scene. During the 1870's and 1880's he came to despair of the prospects of building a separate nationality in North America; by 1891, having witnessed the collapse of so many of his hopes, he concluded that the only solution to the problems besetting Canada was her incorporation into the American union.

His fundamental argument was starkly simple: because of the tremendous geographical obstacles that separated the regions of Canada, the fatal ethnic feud that divided French and English-speaking Canadians, and the steady assimilation of the cultural, social and economic life of English Canada to prevailing American patterns, the desire to preserve a Canada independent of the United States was fated to fail. The attempt to defy geography and artificially force commerce to flow in an east-west direction only stultified development; to hold the disparate regions together by political devices only corrupted public life. As Smith saw it, there were only three ways out of the impasse and frustrations of the late 1880's. Two of these he rejected out of hand: continued dependence upon Britain was incompatible with the pride of a free

9

and self-reliant people; imperial federation was too nebulous in its plans and generally retrogressive. Only incorporation into the United States would bring prosperity, decrease the chances of war between the United States and Britain, and hence pave the way for an ultimate reunion of the Anglo-Saxon race. Though imprecise about exactly how and when this union would be achieved, Smith endorsed free trade between the two countries as a step in the right direction. This, in substance, was the argument that Canadian nationalists felt themselves called upon to repudiate.

The most revealing and effective reactions to Smith's contentions were offered by two Canadian imperialists, G. M. Grant and G. R. Parkin. Grant was born in Nova Scotia in 1835, educated at Glasgow University, and was minister at St Matthew's Church in Halifax until he became Principal of Queen's in 1877. Unlike some other devotees of imperial unity, Grant admired Smith and shared his views about the role of intellectuals in politics and his hope that Canada would become an interpreter within the Anglo-American system. But Grant was a passionate nationalist and some of his expectations were truly visionary. Long before the Canadian Pacific Railway had been completed he had travelled across the country and his record of that journey, *Ocean to Ocean* (1873), was a declaration of faith that in the future Canada would become one of the most populous and powerful nations in the world. He was one of the first major religious figures to endorse the idea that one day all of the churches in the Dominion, including the Catholic, would unite into a national church and thereby provide a model and example for the unity of Christendom. Grant's assessment of *Canada and the Canadian Question* and his rejection of continentalism also ultimately rested on faith. He pointed out how Smith's penchant for the

witty epigram led him to convey false impressions, and he took issue with particular and specific errors; but the burden of his review was that physical geography was not the sole determining influence in the moulding of nations, that traditions and ideals which inspired a people were the primary forces in history, and that the constant and repetitive emphasis upon the material advantages of economic union was repugnant and beneath contempt.

Grant's argument, like Canadian national sentiment of the period, was negative in the sense that it dwelt upon the reasons for rejecting continental union and yet held out only a hope and faith for the future. It was George Parkin who carried the imperialist argument far beyond that point and offered, in his *Imperial Federation The Problem of National Unity* (1892), the most comprehensive case ever penned for imperial unity. Born in 1846, and educated at the University of New Brunswick and Oxford, Parkin's conception of the Empire was a product of his experience. In 1889 he had made a tour of Australia, New Zealand and Canada as a spokesman of the Imperial Federation League, and his travels reinforced his conviction that the instruments of modern technology and communications made the union of the Empire just as possible as the Confederation of Canada. Parkin's imperialism, presented in capsule form in an article in 1888, "The Reorganization of the British Empire," was solidly grounded upon the considerations of geopolitics and power. Canada, to him, was the keystone to the entire imperial system. Her excellent harbours and coal supplies on the east and west coasts; the C.P.R. which provided safe communication to India and Australasia; the wheatlands of the west and the river system joining them to the Atlantic—these to Parkin were the fundamental determinants of the central role that Canada must play in the

Empire. If she were lost to the Empire, he once said, British power would fall by half; but, equally, Canada was dependent upon that power for her survival. Again and again Parkin warned that the two major states of the future would be the United States and Russia, and that if Britain and the Dominion did not somehow combine and co-operate then Britain would lose her predominance and Canada, set adrift, would live in a world which had little respect or regard for minor powers.

There was an ambiguity about Parkin's imperialism. The subtitle of his book—The Problem of National Unity—suggested that the British Empire was the national unit that was the centre of his attenion. Moreover, much of that book was taken up with showing how important imperial federation was from the British point of view. Apart from the seven years he spent as Principal of Upper Canada College in Toronto, Parkin lived much of his later life in England: from 1902 till 1919 he was the Organizing Secretary of the Rhodes Scholarship Trust. It may well be asked whether or not he was more interested in British national interest than in Canadian interests, or does his argument reveal that on important matters these two things were identical or at least complementary?

There was one further consideration which Parkin raised more explicity than any other imperialist—and this related to the place of the French Canadian community in the new order in imperial relations. All imperialists were either unwilling or unable to recognize the French Canadians as anything more than a picturesque, unprogressive and potentially troublesome minority group with certain privileges guaranteed by imperial legislation. They displayed a variety of attitudes towards this minority, attitudes which ranged from D'Alton McCarthy's view that "special privileges" should be confined to

one province only, to Parkin's assurances that the French Canadians were becoming, in relative terms, a smaller and less potent factor in Canadian politics, and that in basic decisions about the country's future they would of necessity have to accept the will of the majority. In addition to this conclusion, Parkin's general interpretation of the French Canadian and his character scarcely leaves any room for wondering why imperialism was so repugnant to French Canadians.

"Anti-Americanism" was fundamental to the imperialist way of thinking. Imperialists dwelt at length upon Canada's need for British support against the dominance of the United States on the continent, and whenever they attempted to outline the advantages of imperial unity they invariably dilated either upon the threatening character of the American presence or the weaknesses of American society, or both. They did so, especially in periods of crisis and insecurity, because it seemed axiomatic to them that without the imperial connection Canada must inexorably come under the domination of the United States and ultimately be annexed to it. In a negative sense then, another argument for imperialism was the depiction of what Canadians would lose if they joined the Republic. It is indicative of the paranoid character of some of the critiques of American life that appeared in the later 1880's and early 1890's that the selection reprinted below may be described as moderate. Written by Castell Hopkins, a prolific journalist and at that time the secretary of the Imperial Federation League in Canada, it was designed to show Americans why Canadians were not entranced with the prospects of annexation. Few imperialists were so vitriolic in their reaction to the United States as Colonel George T. Denison: Chicago, he once warned a friend, was filled with bad water, disease and ruffians. A cavalry officer by training and temperament, Denison was

noted for his threat to meet all annexation-
ists (and he defined these very broadly) on
horseback with his sword. He thought almost
exclusively in military terms and frequently
saw the world through a haze of conspira-
torial fantasies. Denison's preoccupation with
military power was obvious in his impressions
of the position of England in 1897: unde-
ceived by the glamour of the Jubilee celebrations he saw a great weakness in Britain's
dependence upon potentially hostile nations
for food supply. Characteristically, he contended that the heart of the Empire should
be strengthened, not because of his solici-
tude for Englishmen, but because he was
convinced that the insularity and blindness
of the Little Englanders were sources of
weakness to the Empire—an Empire which
was the possession of Canadians as much
as any other people in any part of it. One
of the curious features of Denison's imperial
outlook was that he was as impatient of
supercilious Englishmen as he was vehement
in portraying the corruption of American
society.

During the early 1900's the spectre of
continentalism receded, the wheat boom in-
stilled a sense of optimism, and more and
more Canadian imperialists came to insist
that the time for a fundamental decision on
imperial relations was at hand. In few places
was this enthusiasm and earnestness convey-
ed more pungently than in Stephen Leacock's plea for Canadians to realize the
greatness of their imperial destiny. Now remembered chiefly as a humourist, Leacock
was deadly serious in his devotion to the
imperial ideal in the pre-war years: there
was no more illuminating illustration of the
essentially anti-colonial fervour of that persuasion in this period than his denunciation,
by implication, of those who were satisfied
with being protected either by the Americans
or the British and who were contented with

puny, provincial concerns. During these
years, the imperial problem was a military
and naval problem and upon its solution
depended the role that Canada would play
in world politics and how she would acquire
influence over foreign policy. In 1909
George Foster, a friend of Parkin's since
college days, a member of Macdonald's
cabinet, and later Minister of Trade and
Commerce under Borden, presented his
famous resolution on naval defence to the
House of Commons with a speech which
elaborated the imperialist position. War and
conflict were ever present realities in international relations; Canada could no longer
plead, not, that is, if she were to make good
her claim to nationhood, that she was pre-
occupied with internal developments and
could not afford such preparations. Canada
had been defended by British sea-power for
over a century: this in fact had been the
precondition for her emergence as a nation.
To say that she would continue to be protected in this way appeared to all imperialists as the quintessence of colonialism. It was
not only tantamount to saying that Canadians must remain a dependent people, it
was also, warned William Grant, based
upon a failure to understand the interdependence of nations in the modern world.
For William Grant, who was G. M. Grant's
son and G. R. Parkin's son-in-law, imperialism was but a step toward the establishment of international order.

The critics were not so certain: was not
all this talk of "contributions" suggestive
that imperialists were really colonially-
minded men who were more worried about
Britain, their psychological "homeland," than
Canada? The Canadian imperialists certainly
did not think so: why they believed themselves to be the custodians of the only valid
Canadian nationalism should be clear from
the following passages.

Goldwin Smith, "The Political History of Canada," *The Nineteenth Century* XX (July, 1886) pp. 14-18, 29-31; and *Canada and the Canadian Question*, (Toronto, Hunter, Rose & Co., 1891) pp. 1-3, 54-56, 207, 211, 213-215, 221, 224, 267-70, 274, 278-80.

In order to reproduce the substance of Smith's case as succinctly as possible, selections from the above article have been integrated with selections from the book. Those taken from the article have been placed within brackets.

The Challenge of Continentalism

Whoever wishes to know what Canada is, and to understand the Canadian question, should begin by turning from the political to the natural map. The political map displays a vast and unbroken area of territory, extending from the boundary of the United States up to the North Pole, and equalling or surpassing the United States in magnitude. The physical map displays four separate projections of the cultivable and habitable part of the Continent into arctic waste. The four vary greatly in size, and one of them is very large. They are, beginning from the east, the Maritime Provinces— Nova Scotia, New Brunswick, and Prince Edward Island; Old Canada, comprising the present Provinces of Quebec and Ontario; the newly-opened region of the North-West, comprising the Province of Manitoba and the districts of Alberta,

Athabasca, Assiniboia, and Saskatchewan; and British Columbia. The habitable and cultivable parts of these blocks of territory are not contiguous, but are divided from each other by great barriers of nature, wide and irreclaimable wildernesses or manifold chains of mountains. The Maritime Provinces are divided from Old Canada by the wilderness of many hundred miles through which the Intercolonial Railway runs, hardly taking up a passenger or a bale of freight by the way. Old Canada is divided from Manitoba and the North-West by the great freshwater sea of Lake Superior, and a wide wilderness on either side of it. Manitoba and the North-West again are divided from British Columbia by a triple range of mountains, the Rockies, the Selkirks, and the Golden or Coast range. Each of the blocks, on the other hand, is closely connected by nature, physically and economically, with that portion of the habitable and cultivable continent to the south of it which it immediately adjoins, and in which are its natural markets—the Maritime Provinces, with Maine and the New England States; Old Canada, with New York and with Pennsylvania, from which she draws her coal; Manitoba and the North-West, with Minnesota and Dakota, which share with her the Great Prairie; British Columbia, with the States of the Union on the Pacific. Between the divisions of the Dominion there is hardly any natural trade, and but little even of forced trade has been called into existence under a stringent system of protection. . . . Between the two provinces of Old Canada, though there is no physical barrier, there is an ethnological barrier of the strongest kind, one being British, the other thoroughly French, while the antagonism of race is intensified by that of religion. Such is the real Canada. Whether the four

blocks of territory constituting the Dominion can for ever be kept by political agencies united among themselves and separate from their Continent, of which geographically, economically, and with the exception of Quebec ethnologically, they are parts, is the Canadian question. . . .

[Canada is called a British colony, and over all her provinces waves the British flag. But as soon as you approach her for the purpose of Imperial Federation you will be reminded that a large part of her is French. Not only is it French, but it is becoming more French daily, and at the same time increasing in magnitude. . . . The French are shouldering the British out of the city of Quebec, where not more than six thousand British inhabitants are now left, and out of the Eastern Townships, which have hitherto been a British district; they are encroaching on the British province of Ontario, as well as overflowing into the adjoining states of the Union. The population multiplies apace. There, as in Ireland, the Church encourages early marriage, and does not teach thrift; and were it not for the ready egress into the States, we might have Irish congestion and misery in French Canada. Had French Canada been annexed to the United States, it would no doubt have been absorbed and assimilated, like other alien nationalities, by that vast mass of English-speaking population. As it is, instead of being absorbed or assimilated, the French element rather absorbs and assimilates. Highland regiments disbanded in French Canada have become French. In time, apparently, there will hardly be anything British left in the province of Quebec, except the commercial quarter of Montreal, where the more energetic and mercantile race holds its ground. Had the conqueror freely used his power at first, when the

French numbered only about sixty thousand, New France might have been made English; but its nationality has been fostered under the British flag, and in that respect the work of conquest has been undone. It is difficult indeed, if Canada remains separate from the United States, to see what the limits of French extension will be.

French Canada (now the province of Quebec) is a curious remnant of the France before the Revolution. The peasantry retain with their *patois* the pre-revolutionary character, though, of the allegiance once shared between the king, the seigneur, and the priest, almost the whole is now paid to the priest. There were seigneuries with vexatious feudal incidents; but these have been abolished, not by legislative robbery, in which the rude Canadian is inexpert, but by honest commutation. The people are a simple, kindly, and courteous race, happy on little, clad in homespun, illiterate, unprogressive, pious, priest-ridden, and, whether from fatalism or from superstition, averse to vaccination, whereby they brought upon themselves and their neighbours the other day a fearful visitation of small-pox. They are all small, very small farmers; and, looking down from the citadel of Quebec upon the narrow slips of land with their river fronts on the St. Lawrence, you see that here, as in old France, subdivision has been carried to an extreme.

It has been said that the Spaniards colonised for gold, the English for freedom, the French for religion. New France, at all events, was religious, and it has kept the character which the Jesuit missionary impressed on it. The Church is very strong and very rich. Virtually it is established, since to escape tithe you must avow yourself a Protestant. Clerical influence is tremendously powerful. . . . It is

due to the clergy to say that they seem to make the people moral, though in ecclesiastical fashion. What they deem immorality they put down with a high hand; they restrain dancing and thunder against opéra bouffe. The Church has a strong hold on the peasant's heart through its ceremonial, which is the only pageantry or poetry of peasant life. Till lately the Church of French Canada was Gallican, and lived, like the old national Church of France, on perfectly good terms with the State. But now comes the Jesuit, with the Encyclical and the declaration of Papal Infallibility in his hand. There is a struggle between Jesuitism and Gallicanism under the walls of the citadel of Gallicanism, the great Sulpician Seminary at Montreal. The Jesuit, having all the influences of the day upon his side, prevails. A new chapter of history is opened and troubles begin between Church and State. . . .

The conqueror might have suppressed French nationality. Instead of this, he preserved and protected it. He gave the conquered a measure of his own liberty, and perhaps as large a measure as at that time they who had known nothing but absolute government could bear. He gave them a representative assembly, trial by jury, Habeas Corpus, an administration generally pure in place of one which was scandously corrupt, deliverance from oppressive imposts, and an appeal in case of misgovernment to Parliament instead of Pompadour. He gave them liberty of opinion and introduced among them the printing press. The one successful colony of France owes its success to British tutelage. French writers are fain to acknowledge this, and if some of them complain because the half-measure of liberty was not a whole measure, and the conquering race kept power in its own hands, the answer is that conquest is conquest, and that the monarchy of Louis the Fourteenth was neither unaggressive nor invariably liberal to the vanquished. . . . The Englishman in Canada has in the main got on perfectly well with the conquered Frenchman; even if there has been sometimes political antagonism between them, their social relations have been good. The French fought for England in the revolutionary war, and again in the war of 1812. If the hostile attitude of the Puritans of New England towards their religion decided them in the first case, it can hardly have decided them in the second; at least, the rule under which they had lived in the interim can hardly have been oppressive. It was one of their leaders, Etienne Taché, who said that the last gun fired in favour of British dominion on the continent would be fired by a French Canadian. The late Sir George Cartier, the political chief of French Canada in his day, was proud to call himself a British subject speaking French. . . .

There is, I believe, no feeling whatever among the French Canadians against England. But French nationality grows daily more intense and daily finds more political as well as literary expression. We had trouble with it the other day, when Quebec sympathised on national grounds with the rising of the French half-breeds under Riel in the North-West, as she had with previous attempts to secure that vast realm for the French race and religion. Regiments from Quebec were sent to the theatre of war, but they were not sent to the front. . . .]

. . . Not only has New France shown no increase of tendency to merge her nationality in that of the Dominion; her tendency has been directly the other way. She has recently . . . unfurled her national flag, and at the same time placed herself

as the French Canadian nation, under the special protection of the Pope, who accepts the position of her ecclesiastical lord. At her head, and to all appearances firmly seated in power, is the chief of the Nationalist and Papal party, who bids Blue and Red blend themselves in the tricolor and restores to the Jesuits their estates. The old Bleu or Conservative party, associated with the clergy of the Gallican school, which by its union with the Tories in the British provinces linked Quebec politically to the Dominion, has fallen, as it seems, to rise no more. What life is left in it is sustained largely by Dominion subsidies of which the Ottawa Government makes it the accredited channel. "The complete autonomy of the French Canadian nationality and the foundation of a French Canadian and Catholic state, having for its mission to continue in America the glorious work of our ancestors," are the avowed aims of the Nationalist and Ultramontane press. Greybeards of the old Conservative school protest that all this means nothing, that no design of autonomy has been formed, and that it is unjust to speak of French nationality and theocracy as dangers to Confederation. Whether the design has been distinctly formed or not matters little if the tendency is manifestly there and is gaining strength every day. Let those who prophesy to us smooth things take stock of the facts. When one community differs from another in race, language, religion, character, spirit, social structure, aspirations, occupying also a territory apart, it is a separate nation, and is morally certain to pursue a different course, let it designate itself as it can. French Canada may be ultimately absorbed in the English-speaking population of a vast Continent; amalgamate with British Canada so as to form a united nation it apparently never can. . . .

From British as well as from French Canada there is a constant flow of emigration to the richer country, and the great centres of employment. Dakota and the other new States of the American West are full of Canadian farmers; the great American cities are full of Canadian clerks and men of business, who usually make for themselves a good name. It is said that in Chicago there are 25,000. Hundreds of thousands of Canadians have relatives in the United States. Canadians in great numbers—it is believed as many as 40,000—enlisted in the American army during the civil war. There is a Lodge of the Grand Army at Ottawa. A young Canadian thinks no more of going to push his fortune in New York or Chicago than a young Scotchman thinks of going to Manchester or London. The same is the case in the higher callings as in the lower: clergymen, those of the Church of England as well as those of other churches, freely accept calls to the other side of the Line. So do professors, teachers, and journalists. The Canadian churches are in full communion with their American sisters, and send delegates to each other's Assemblies. Cadets educated at a Military College to command the Canadian army against the Americans, have gone to practise as Civil Engineers in the United States. The Benevolent and National Societies have branches on both sides of the Line, and hold conventions in common. Even the Orange Order has now its lodges in the United States, where the name of President is substituted in the oath for that of the Queen. American labour organizations . . . extend to Canada. The American Science Association met the other day at Toronto. All the re-

forming and philanthropic movements, such as the Temperance movement, the Women's Rights' movement, and the Labour movements, with their conventions, are continental. Intermarriages between Canadians and Americans are numerous, so numerous as scarcely to be remarked. Americans are the chief owners of Canadian mines, and large owners of Canadian timber limits. The railway system of the continent is one. The winter ports of Canada are those of the United States. Canadian banks trade largely in the American market, and some have branches there. There is almost a currency union, American bank-bills commonly passing at par in Ontario, while those of remote Canadian Provinces pass at par only by special arrangement. American gold passes at par, while silver coin is taken at a small discount: in Winnipeg even the American nickel is part of the common currency. The Dominion bank-bills, though payable in gold, are but half convertible, because what the Canadian banks want is not British but American gold. Canadians go to the American watering-places, while Americans pass the summer on Canadian lakes. Canadians take American periodicals, to which Canadian writers often contribute. They resort for special purchases to New York stores, or even those of the Border cities. Sports are international; so are the Base Ball organisations; and the Toronto "Nine" is recruited in the States. All the New-World phrases and habits are the same on both sides of the Line. The two sections of the English-speaking race on the American continent, in short, are in a state of economic, intellectual, and social fusion, daily becoming more complete. Saving the special connection of a limited circle with the Old Country, Ontario is an American State of the Northern type, cut off from its sisters by a customs line, under a separate government and flag. . . .

To force trade into activity between the Provinces and turn it away from the United States, giving the Canadian farmer a home market, and consolidating Canadian nationality at the same time, were the ostensible objects of the adoption in 1879 of a Protective tariff. The real object perhaps was at least as much to capture the manufacturer's vote and his contributions to the election fund of the party in power. . . .

The isolation of the different Canadian markets from each other, and the incompatibility of their interests, add in their case to the evils and absurdities of the protective system. What is meat to one Province is, even on the protectionist hypothesis, poison to another. Ontario was to be forced to manufacture; she has no coal; yet to reconcile Nova Scotia to the tariff a coal duty was imposed; in vain, for Ontario after all continued to import her coal from Pennsylvania. Manitoba and the North-West produced no fruit; yet they were compelled to pay a duty in order to protect the fruit-grower of Ontario 1500 miles away. Hardest of all was the lot of the North-West farmer. His natural market, wherein to buy farm implements, was in the neighbouring cities of the United States, where, moreover, implements were made most suitable to the prairie. But to force him to buy in Eastern Canada 25 per cent was laid on farm implements. As he still bought in the States, the 25 per cent was made 35 per cent. . . .

Without commercial intercourse or fusion of population, the unity produced by a mere political arrangement can hardly be strong or deep. It will, for the most part, be confined to the politicians,

or to those directly interested in the work of Dominion parties. . . .

In the want of a real bond among the members of Confederation, the anti-national attitude of Quebec, the absence of real Dominion parties, and the consequent difficulty of holding the Dominion together and finding a basis for the administration must be found the excuse, if any excuse can be found, for the system of politicial corruption which during the last twenty years has prevailed. "Better Terms," that is, increased subsidies to Provinces from the Dominion treasury, Dominion grants for local railways and other local works and concessions to contractors, together with the patronage including . . . appointments to the Senate, have been familiar engines of government. . . .

. . . The Government, which, it is justly said, ought in the matter of public works to act as trustee for the whole people, in effect proclaims that public works will be regulated by the interest of constituencies whose support it receives. That "the whole North-West of Canada has been used as one vast bribery fund" is a statement just made by a leading member of the Opposition, who can point to at least one recent and most flagrant instance in proof of his sweeping accusation. But what corruption can be more pestilential or more dangerous to the commonwealth than the surrender of the commercial policy of the country to private interests, in return for their votes and the support of their money in elections? . . .

[The thread of political connection is wearing thin. This England sees, and the consequence is a recoil which has produced a movement in favour of Imperial Federation. It is proposed not only to arrest the process of gradual emancipa-

tion, but to reverse it and to reabsorb the colonies into the unity of the Empire. No definite plan has been propounded, indeed, any demand for a plan is deprecated, and we are adjured to embrace the principle of the scheme and leave the details for future revelation—to which we must answer that the principle of a scheme is its object, and that it is impossible to determine whether the object is practically attainable without a working plan. There is no one in whose eyes the bond between the colonies and the mother country is more precious than it is in mine. Yet I do not hesitate to say that, so far as Canada is concerned, Imperial Federation is a dream. The Canadian people will never part with their self-government. Their tendency is entirely the other way. They have recently . . . asserted their fiscal independence, and by instituting a Supreme Court of their own, they have evinced a disposition to withdraw as much as they can of their affairs from the jurisdiction of the Privy Council. Every association, to make it reasonable and lasting, must have some practical object. The practical objects of Imperial Federation would be the maintenance of common armaments and the establishment of a common tariff. But to neither of these, I am persuaded, would Canada ever consent; she would neither contribute to Imperial armaments nor conform to an Imperial tariff. Though her people are brave and hardy, they are not, any more than the people of the United States, military, nor could they be brought to spend their earnings in Asiatic or African wars. . . . Remember that Canada is only in part British. The commercial and fiscal circumstances of the colony again are as different as possible from those of the mother country. . . .

Why not leave the connection as it

is? Because, reply the advocates of Imperial Federation, the connection will not remain as it is; the process of separation will go on and the attenuated tie will snap. Apart from this not unreasonable apprehension, there are, so far as I know, only two reasons against acquiescence in the present system. One of these may be thought rather vague and intangible. It is that the spirit of a dependency, even of a dependency enjoying the largest measure of self-government, is never that of a nation, and that we can make Englands only in the way in which England herself was made. The other is more tangible, and is brought home to us at this moment by the dispute with the Americans about the Fisheries. The responsibility of Great Britain for the protection of her distant colony is not easily discharged to the distant colony's satisfaction. To Canadians, as to other people, their own concerns seem most important; they forget what the Imperial country has upon her hands in all parts of the globe; they have an unlimited idea of her power; and they expect her to put forth the whole force of the Empire in defence of Canadian fishing rights, while perhaps at the same moment Australians are calling upon her to put forth the whole force of the Empire in defence of their claims upon New Guinea. Confiding in Imperial support, they perhaps take stronger ground and use more bellicose language than they otherwise would. But the more democratic England becomes, the more impossible will it be to get her people to go to war for any interests but their own. The climax of practical absurdity would be reached if England were involved in war by some quarrel arising out of the Canadian customs duties, imposed partly to protect Canadian manufacturers against British goods. . . . .]

Annexation is an ugly word; it seems to convey the idea of force or pressure applied to the smaller State, not of free, equal, and honourable union, like that between England and Scotland. Yet there is no reason why the union of the two sections of the English-speaking people on this Continent should not be as free, as equal, and as honourable as the union of England and Scotland. We should rather say their reunion than their union, for before their unhappy schism they were one people. Nothing but the historical accident of a civil war ending in secession, instead of amnesty, has made them two. . . .

That a union of Canada with the American Commonwealth, like that into which Scotland entered with England, would in itself be attended with great advantages cannot be questioned, whatever may be the considerations on the other side or the reasons for delay. It would give to the inhabitants of the whole Continent as complete a security for peace and immunity from war taxation as is likely to be attained by any community or group of communities on this side of the Millenium. Canadians almost with one voice say that it would greatly raise the value of property in Canada; in other words, that it would bring with it a great increase of prosperity. . . .

On the other hand, there is the affection of the Colonists for the mother country, which has always been kind to them in intention, even if she has not had the power to defend their rights and her interference has ceased to be useful. This might prevail if union with the rest of the race on this Continent, under the sanction of the mother country, would really be a breach of affection for her. But it would be none. It would be no more a breach of affection than the naturalisation, now fully recognised by Brit-

ish law, of multitudes both of Englishmen and of Canadians in the United States. Let us suppose that the calamitous rupture of the last century had never taken place, that the whole race on this Continent had remained united, and had parted, when the time came, from the mother country in peace; where would the outrage on love or loyalty have been? Admitted into the councils of their own Continent, and exercising their fair share of influence there, Canadians would render the mother country the best of all services, and the only service in their power, by neutralising the votes of her enemies. Unprovoked hostility on the part of the American Republic to Great Britain would then become impossible. . . .

Nor need Canada give up any of the distinctive character or historical associations which she has preserved through the continuance of her connection with the mother country. . . . The Federal system admits wide local diversities, and if Ontario or Nova Scotia clings to the British statute-book, to the British statute-book it may cling. There is no reason even why Canadians, who like to show their spirit by military celebrations, should not celebrate Canadian victories as the Scotch celebrate Bannockburn. Americans would smile. Of the antipathy to Americans sedulously kept up within select circles and in certain interests, there is absolutely none among the Canadian people at large. It would be strange if there were any, considering that half of them have brothers, sons, or cousins on the American side of the Line. . . .

Again, Canadians who heartily accept democracy wish that there should be two experiments in it on this Continent rather than one, and the wish is shared by thoughtful Americans not a few. But we have seen that in reality the two

experiments are not being made. Universal suffrage and party government are the same, and their effects are the same in both Republics. Differences there are, such as that between the Presidential and the Cabinet system, of a subordinate kind, yet not unimportant, and such as might make it worthwhile to forego for a time at least the advantages of union, supposing that the dangers and economical evils of separation were not too great, and if the territorial division were not extravagantly at variance with the fiat of Nature. The experiments of politicial science must be tried with some reference to terrestrial convenience. Besides, those who scan the future without prejudice must see that the political fortunes of the Continent are embarked in the great Republic, and that Canada will best promote her own ultimate interests by contributing without unnecessary delay all that she has in the way of political character and force towards the saving of the main chance and the fulfilment of the common hope. The native American element in which the tradition of self-government resides is hard pressed by the foreign element untrained to self-government, and stands in need of the reinforcement which the entrance of Canada into the Union would bring it. . . .

There is a conflict of forces, and we must judge each for himself which are the primary forces and likely to prevail. Prevail the primary forces will in the end, however long their action may be suspended by a number of secondary forces arrayed against them. In the case of German and in that of Italian unity the number and strength of the secondary forces arrayed against the event were such, and the action of the great forces was so long suspended by them, that it seemed even to sagacious observers as if the event

would never come. It came, irresistible and irreversible, and we see now that Bismarck and Cavour were the ministers of destiny.

In the present case there are, on one side, geography, commerce, identity of race, language, and institutions, which with the mingling of population and constant intercourse of every kind, acting in ever-increasing intensity, have brought about a general fusion, leaving no barriers standing but the political and fiscal lines. On the other side, there is British and Imperial sentiment, which, however, is confined to the British, excluding the French and Irish and other nationalities, and even among the British is livelier as a rule among the cultivated and those whose minds are steeped in history than among those who are working for their bread; while to set against it there is the idea, which can hardly fail to make way, of a great continent with an almost unlimited range of production forming the home of a united people, shutting out war and presenting the field as it would seem for a new and happier development of humanity. Again, there are bodies of men, official, political, and commercial, whose interests are bound up with the present state of things, whose feelings naturally go with those interests, who in many cases suffer little from the economical consequences of isolation, and who, gathered in the capital or in the great cities exercise an influence out of proportion to their numbers on public opinion and its organs. . . .

. . . However, if the primary forces are working towards an event, sooner or later the crisis arrives; the man appears, and the bidding of Destiny is done.

G. M. Grant, Review of *Canada and the Canadian Question,* "Second Notice," *The Week,* (May 15, 1891), pp. 380-82.

In Defence of Canada

The main position of the book is that the political unification of the continent would be to the advantage of Canada, of the United States, and of Great Britain. . . . To this everything else in his book is subsidiary, including the attempts to prove, by appeals to geography, economics and history, as well as to the etiquette maintained at Rideau Hall, that Confederation was a mistake. He believes that the great "primary" forces will in the end triumph over the "secondary" ones, which he admits are at present standing in the way of his great ideal. . . .

. . . The present book, in its perpetual insistence on the material prosperity that union would bring, appeals far too much to the baser side of human nature. Surely the lessons that history teaches are that wealth is not the one thing indispensable to a people; that commercial prosperity may be bought at too great a price; that if wealth be gained at the cost of the slightest loss of moral power, it proves not a blessing but a curse that can never be shaken off; and that simplicity of life is not inconsistent with the highest culture any more than with the formation of the noblest character. All this no one would admit more readily than Dr. Goldwin Smith, and he would answer that in his opinion there would be no loss of moral power to Canada in consenting to a union with the States. He must admit, however, that that would depend on the paramount motives that determined the country to such a decision, and that appeals to cupidity or to fear are alike unworthy of a great writer and insulting to a great people. . . .

. . . It is also something like cant to say that "there is no reason why the union of the two sections of English-speaking people on this Continent should not be as free, as equal, and as honourable as the union of England and Scotland," or to speak of "a union of Canada with the American Commonwealth like that into which Scotland entered with England." Such a union is not on the carpet and is totally out of the question. There is no analogy between the two cases. Scotland in consenting to the union forfeited nothing historical or sentimental and therefore no moral force, whereas Canada would forfeit everything. In the one case, there was no disruption from an Empire to which Scotland belonged and therefore no change of citizenship. Scotland remained a distinct realm and has ever since been legislated for distinctly. The two crowns had been on one head ever since she had given her King to England. . . . While she gave up her separate parliament she did not give up the parliamentary system. How different all these things would be in the case of Canada! It is a delusion to fancy that the great Republic could receive us save as a number of separate states, or to fancy that it would accept our monarchial, judi-

cial, or parliamentary system, our name, our flag or our citizenship. . . . The democracy of the United States is too thoroughly convinced of its own superiority to the rest of the world and too sure that Canada must, in due season, fall into its mouth like a ripe plum to listen to any Treaty of Union such as that to which Scotland and England agreed. Every letter or leading article on this side of the line in favour of union deepens these natural convictions or delusions of the democracy of the States, and it may therefore be said that the Canadian advocates of Continental Union are its most scientific opponents. Three things we would be called upon to sacrifice at the outset. In the first place, our citizenship. Ceasing to be British, we would become citizens of an alien, possibly a hostile nation. . . . This implies no disparagement, on our part, of the American people. On the contrary, we heartily subscribe to what is said with regard to community of citizenship, in the section on Imperial Federation. "There is no apparent reason why, among all the states of our race, there should not be community of citizenship, so that a citizen of any one of the nations might take up the rights of a citizen in any one of the others at once upon his change of domicile, and without the process of naturalization. This would be political unity of no inconsiderable kind without diplomatic liabilities, or the strain, which surely no one can think free from peril, of political centralization." . . . The objections to such a proposal would not come from Britain, Canada or Australia. Even as it is, there is nothing offensive in the British oath of allegiance. The throwing away by us of our British citizenship would however be a strange introduction to this proposed bringing in of a wider franchise. In the second place, we would

have to sacrifice our country. To be a Canadian now is to be something more than a Nova Scotian or an Ontarian. It is simply not true that "no inhabitant of Nova Scotia or New Brunswick calls himself a Canadian," . . .

. . . Yes, "we Canadians," to use the phrase of young Nova Scotia, set out in 1867 to make a country, and to make it on British lines because we were all British to begin with. In our inspiring work of nation-building, mistakes no doubt have been committed. Where is the man, outside of the editorial sanctum, who has never blundered? Where the nation that has never been led astray? But we have always felt that the country would survive in spite of the mistakes into which politicians might drift. In 1867, anti-confederates pointed out that the proposed Dominion consisted of four divisions that could not be united together by railways and each of which was intended by nature to be a mere appendage to a corresponding State or section to the South. There was a measure of truth in this. But the people would not listen. Instinctively they understood that every nation must be ready to pay a price, must be willing to transcend difficulties in order to realize itself, to maintain its independence, to secure for itself a distinctive future. They said, let us rise up and build. So, they added to their unequalled system of internal navigation from the Straits of Belle Isle up into the centre of the continent, an unparalleled railway system along lines where engineers and scientific men had declared that railways could not be built. And now, when the difficulties have been overcome, when every part of our confederacy is linked together by bands of the best steel, when magnificent dry docks have been built at Halifax and Vancouver, when our coasts and rivers and lakes have

been lighted with hundreds of lighthouses, now, when—after incredible toil and expense and faith on the part of, comparatively speaking, a handful of people scattered over half a continent—we have succeeded in building our nation's house, it is coolly proposed that we should break it into fragments as if it were a card castle and as if the putting of it together had been merely a bit of child's play on the part of grown babies! How can anyone fancy that such a thing is possible! In the third place, we would have to sacrifice our Constitution. . . . It is Parliamentary, after the British model which has been imitated by every other free country, whereas "The framers of the American Constitution were full of Montesquieu's false notion about the necessity of entirely separating the executive from the legislative." A sovereign authority above the Provinces gave them certain powers, whereas the framers of the American Constitution were forced to content themselves with such powers for the Central Government as a number of Sovereign States were willing to concede. It would take too long to go over the points of difference, one by one, and to show the superiority of our system in every particular, save in the matter of subsidies to the Provinces. . . . [A nation's] Constitution is not a coat to be thrown aside for a neighbour's, but the very body which the inner life has gathered round it from the past and the present. This outward form can be slowly changed by development to meet the changing environment and the growth of ideas, but it cannot be exchanged for another by revolution without grievous—perhaps irreparable—hurt to the nation's life.

This bare enumeration of what Canada would have to surrender in order to unite with the Republic is sufficient to make us wonder that anyone could fancy

such a thing to be within the bounds of possibility. What counterbalancing gains are mentioned? First, commercial development. This is the one strong point that is made. That "the near market must, as a rule, be the best," seems to most men plain as daylight. But that a nation should sell itself for this is inconceivable. . . . Another gain that appeals to Christian sentiment is mentioned. "Those who scan the future without prejudice must see that the political fortunes of the Continent are embarked in the great Republic, and that Canada will best promote her own ultimate interests by contributing without unnecessary delay all that she has in the way of political character and force towards the saving of the main chance and the fulfilment of the common hope. The native American element, in which the tradition of self-government resides, is hard pressed by the foreign element untrained to self-government, and stands in need of the reinforcement which the entrance of Canada into the Union would bring it." There is something in this, and I wish to admit it frankly and to acknowledge the force with which it is put. It gives no pleasure to any sane man to hear of a threatened war of races in the South, or of anarchism in Chicago, or of any other evil force threatening American civilization. But, it is clear that no moral contribution which we could bring to the Republic would ever amount to anything if we commenced by being false to ourselves or to that Empire, which is the great power representing liberty, peace, righteousness and commercial freedom to all lands; still less, if it could be said that we were prompted to union by the hope of securing the "cash value" of the Republic's markets or by a political cowardice and indolence that sought to escape the trouble of settling our own internal difficulties. . . .

. . . "The moral federation of the whole English-speaking race throughout the world" is the vision that inspires those who plead for closer union with the Mother Country as against separation, but they are profoundly convinced that the steps to it must be taken along the lines of their own historical development. British statesmen have also probably learnt—at least the author of "Canada and the Canadian Question" once hoped that they had learnt—"the vanity of attempting by unreciprocated demonstrations of good will and caresses which are invariably misconstrued to gain the friendship of the one nation on earth whose friendship is not to be gained." This is much stronger language than I would care to use, but I am none the less convinced that the best way to gain the friendship of the United States—and we all wish to gain it—is by preserving our own self-respect and maintaining our own rights. At any rate, disunion is not a good step to take on the way to union, and concession is a better policy in dealing with weakness than in dealing with hate. . . .

Dr. Goldwin Smith once said that "few have fought against geography and prevailed." Man triumphs continually over geography or nature in any form. Every trans-continental railway is such a triumph. The unity of the Swiss, the union of the Highlands and Lowlands, of Celts and Saxons in what I will call—*pace* Dr. Goldwin Smith—the Scottish nation, are other examples. Would it not be more to the purpose to ask, how few have fought against human nature, especially against its best elements, and prevailed? . . .

. . . The average Canadian is now prepared to ask, and perhaps with a little amazement, what hinders us from proceeding along our old lines? The answer of the author will probably be the one word "Quebec." Great is geography but greater far the Jesuit. Canada's disease was bad enough before but now there is no hope. . . .Let us have patience and remember that the development of a nation is not to be measured by the short span of human life. Last century, all Canada was French. Now, it includes seven provinces, six of them English-speaking. In half a century the number of Provinces will probably be doubled and Quebec alone will be French. Already its wisest leaders see that unless their countrymen learn English they must be handicapped for life. . . . Before very long most of the emigration from the northern countries of Europe will be obliged to flow into our North-West, and then into the vacant spaces of the Maritime Provinces neglected now in the eagerness to homestead and preëmpt prairie land. The whole of that immigration will be English-speaking after the first generation. Is not this future as certain as the rising of to-morrow's sun? Will it not be as vain for the Jesuit to fight against it as it was for Canute to bid the tide cease to rise? . . . Naturally and rightly French Canadians have a sentimental attachment to France, but politically they are British and their hearts are all for Canada. When they vote solid it will not be to disgrace their native land or to strike a blow at Britain. There can be no insuperable difficulty in coöperating with a race that has produced in our day men like Cartier, Dorion, Joly, Masson, Taschereau, Frechette, the Casgrains and others like minded who are still in the political arena.

We differ radically, then, from Dr. Goldwin Smith in the main positions of this book. Having cast the horoscope of Canada with the fixed preconception that Confederation must be smashed, he is dissatisfied with everything that makes for

its permanence. The great and the little are seen alike from this one point of view, and his judgments are accordingly one-sided and harsh. . . .

. . . It is no pleasure to criticize a man whom we admire. But in the interest of the country it is necessary to point out that he has erred grievously. He could do such grand work for Canada, if he would only lead us in reforming what should be reformed, one step at a time, instead of insisting that the whole house must be pulled down about our ears. Would it not be wiser to join hands to make the Canada of to-day more united and more worthy of the love of her sons and the respect of her neighbours?

George R. Parkin, "The Reorganization of the British Empire," *The Century,* Vol. XXXVII (Dec. 1888), pp. 188-91.

The Forces of Union

Within a short time a remarkable change has come over public opinion in the British Isles themselves. Twenty years ago it almost seemed as if Great Britain was ready voluntarily to throw away her vast colonial empire. A whole school of politicians favored the idea, and seemed to have gained the public ear. "The Times," supposed to reflect public opinion, claimed that England was paying too high a price for enjoying the luxury of colonial loyalty, and warned the colonies to prepare for the separation that was inevitable.

John Bright's eloquence and Goldwin Smith's literary skill were alike employed in the same direction. Under such guidance, intoxicated by the success of free trade, and indulging in dreams of a cosmopolitan future which it was to produce for the nations, the British people seemed for a time to look upon the colonies as burdens which entailed responsibilities without giving any adequate return. All this has now been changed. John Bright in England and Goldwin Smith in Canada still harp on the old string, but get no response from the popular heart, nor even from political parties. Great Britain has found that she still has to fight for her own hand, commercially and politically, and cannot afford to despise her natural allies. The vigor of colonial life, the expansion of colonial trade and power, the greatness of the part which the colonies are manifestly destined to take in affairs, have impressed even the slow British imagination. The integrity of the empire is fast becoming an essential article in the creed of all political parties. The idea appeals to the instincts of Great Britain's new democracy even more strongly than to the pride of her aristocracy, and with better reason, for the vast unoccupied areas of the empire in the colonies offer to the workingman a field of hope when the pressure at home has become too severe. . . .

To the development of this wider view the growth of the United States has contributed largely. It has illustrated on a large scale the expansive energy of our race where the conditions are favorable. It has enlarged our conception of Anglo-Saxon self-governing capacity. It has shown that an unparalleled impulse to a nation's life may be given by vast breadth of territory with variety of climate and production. On the other hand, the British people see in the American Union proof that immense territorial extent is not incompatible, under modern conditions, with that representative system of popular government which had its birth and development in England and its most notable adaptation in America. They are beginning to believe that their political system will safely bear the strain of still further adaptation to wider areas, if the welfare or necessities of the empire demand a change. That they will demand it

is a proposition now become so evident that it scarcely requires proof. The home population of Great Britain, which alone exercises national functions in their broadest sense, and bears the full burden of national responsibilities, is about thiry-five millions. This number has practically reached its outside limit of expansion. The Anglo-Saxon population of the empire abroad is already about eleven millions, and is increasing rapidly. It is a population which has already grouped itself into communities of national extent, self-governing, self-reliant, progressive, and with a clear sense of the large place which they are destined to fill in the world. The time cannot be very far distant when, by the flux of population and the process of growth, their numbers will equal or surpass those of the people of the British Isles. There can be no question that long before that period has arrived a readjustment of functions and responsibilities will be essential to the maintenance of the empire as a political unit. The British people at home cannot continue to bear alone the increasing burden of imperial duties. Great communities like Australia or Canada would disgrace the traditions of the race if they remained permanently content with anything short of an equal share in the largest possible national life. For both mother land and colonies that largest life will unquestionably be found in organic national unity. The weight of public sentiment throughout the empire is at present strongly in favor of such unity, and national interest recommends it. . . .

With this sentiment, which makes unity possible, the national interest coincides. For the colonies the alternative is independence, when, as small and struggling nationalities, they will have to take their place in a world which has developed distinct tendencies towards the agglomeration of immense states, and where absorption or comparative insignificance can alone await them. For Great Britain the choice is between amalgamating permanently in some way her strength and resources with those of the colonies, or abdicating the relatively foremost place which she now holds among the nations. The growth in population of the United States and the expansion of Russia are already beginning to dwarf by comparison all other nations. Those confined to Europe will, within the next fifty years, be out of the first rank. Great Britain alone, with unlimited room for healthful expansion on other continents, has the possibility of a future equal to the greatest; has the chance of retaining her hegemony as a ruling and civilizing power. Should she throw away the opportunity, her history will be one of arrested development. The process by which her vast colonial empire has come to her has been one of spontaneous growth, the outcome of a decisive national tendency. By inherent inclination the Anglo-Saxon is a trader. The character is one of which we need not feel ashamed. It has been found to consist in our history, with all the fighting energy of the Roman and much of the intellectual energy of the Greek. It does not seem incompatible with the moral energy of Christianity, and furnishes the widest opportunity for its exercise.

It has been under the impulse of this trading instinct that Great Britain has founded empire; to satisfy it, she must maintain empire. Among all the nations of the earth she stands in the unique position of owning by undisputed right immense areas of territory under every climate on the globe, and hence produces, or can produce, within her own national boundaries, all the raw materials of com-

merce. As civilization becomes more complex and more diffused, the products of every clime are, in an increasing ratio, laid under contribution to supply its manifold wants. Every step towards the complete national assimilation of so widespread an empire must favor the free exchange of commodities, with the necessary result of stimulating productive energy and developing latent resources. Every expansion of trade makes the security of trade a matter of increasing importance. For a race of traders, scattered over all quarters of the globe, peace, made secure by resting on organized power, is a supreme interest. The best guarantee of permanent peace that the world could have would be the consolidation of a great oceanic empire, the interests of whose members would lie chiefly in safe commercial intercourse. For filling such a place in the world Great Britain's position is absolutely unique among the nations of history. She holds the chief key to the commerce of the East in the passes of the Mediterranean and the Red seas. She commands an alternative route by the Cape of Good Hope. Across Canada she has yet a third, giving her for many purposes a still closer connection with the extreme East than do the other two. The geographical distribution of the coal areas under her control, and the defended or defensible harbors suitable for coaling stations contiguous to them, are among the most remarkable elements in her incomparable resources for prosecuting or protecting commerce in an age of steam. Already in electric connection with almost every important point in her dominions, her telegraph system only awaits the laying of the proposed cable from British Columbia to Australasia to make that connection complete without touching on foreign soil.

Her widely separated provinces and outlying posts of vantage are thus effectively in touch for mutual support, more than the parts of any of the great nations of the past. She thus unites the comprehensiveness of a world-wide empire with a relative compactness secured by that practical contraction of our planet which has taken place under the combined influences of steam and electricity. No other nation has ever had—it is well-nigh impossible to believe that any other nation ever will have—so commanding a position for exercising the functions of what we have called an oceanic empire, interested in developing and able to protect the commerce of the world. The question of whether she shall permanently retain this position is one of profound international as well as national concern. Above all, for the United States, as a great trading community, kindred in race, language, and, speaking very broadly, in national purpose, it must have a deep and abiding interest. . . .

The development of the United States has proved that the spread of a nation over vast areas, including widely separated States with diverse interests, need not prevent it from becoming strongly bound together in a political organism which combines the advantages of national greatness and unity of purpose with jealously guarded freedom of local self-government. This is in part due to the amazing change which has been effected in the mutual relation of the world's inhabitants by improved means of speedy intercourse. Steam and electricity have re-created the world, and on a more accessible scale. Canada, or even Australia, is now much closer to the center of the British Empire for all practical purposes than were the Western and Pacific States to Washington forty years ago; nearer

even than Scotland was to London one hundred years ago. Under these new conditions there is no sufficient reason for doubting that an empire like that of Great Britain can be held together in bonds as secure as those which bind together great continental states like the United States and Russia, provided that the elements of true national life are present, as they certainly are in this case.

The federation of Great Britain and her colonies would only be an extension of what has already been done on a large scale. The United States are a federation, Germany is a federation, each designed by its framers to obviate the difficulties incident to the administration of a congeries of small states, and for great ends to secure unity of national action. The problem before Great Britain is different, but would seem to be incomparably less difficult than that involved in either of the two cases referred to. In Germany, dynasties and states whose individual existence had been carefully preserved and fondly cherished for centuries long presented an apparently insuperable barrier to union, effected at last only under the strong pressure of external danger and in the enthusiasm of a great and successful struggle for race supremacy. Every student of American history knows the violent prejudices which had to be overcome and the extraordinary effort which it required to organize and gain acceptance for the Federal Constitution, even after the War of Independence had demonstrated the necessity for united action on the part of the various States. Sectional jealousies and rivalries have never been developed to a corresponding extent in the various provinces of the British Empire. For them federation would only be recasting and making more permanent a union which already exists, though under imperfect conditions. Besides this, the operation of the federal principle is now more thoroughly understood; its advantages have been gauged and its difficulties grappled with. The freedom of self-government long enjoyed by the great colonies has developed a strong feeling of local independence; but it has also been the best of all preparations for a wider political organization. Canada and Australia are today as jealous of imperial interference with local legislation as is any State in the Union of unjustified Federal assumptions. But as their autonomy in the control of their own affairs has become admitted and assured, they look without suspicion on the idea of combination having for its purpose the accomplishment of great national ends. These ends have become more manifest with the spread of their commerce to every part of the world, and with the manifold multiplication of national interests. Questions of peace and war; the safety of the great ocean routes; the adjustment of international differences; the relations of trade, currency, communication, emigration—in all these their concern is already large, and becomes larger from year to year. In dealing with all such questions their voice, as component parts of a great empire, will be far more efficient than as struggling independent nationalities. That voice is, in a measure, given to them now by courtesy, and as a necessary concession to their growing importance; but for permanent nationality it must be theirs by ordinary right of citizenship, through full incorporation into the political system of the state, so far as relations with other states are concerned. Those who believe it impracticable to give unity of this kind to the empire underestimate the strength of the influences which make for the continuity of national life. On this continent we see

to-day a sufficiently striking illustration of this strength. We can easily understand that it requires no very marked natural boundary to form a permanent line of separation between nations which differ in language, religion, and descent, as in the case of European states. But in America an almost purely arbitrary line of division has for more than a century served sharply to separate into two nationalities, and across the breadth of a continent, two peoples who are of the same origin, speak the same language, study the same literature, and are without any decisive distinctions of religious creed. The admitted present loyalty of Canada has deepened and matured through a long series of years when the United States were sweeping past them in a career of prosperity almost without example in history, and when union with them seemed as if it would secure for Canada an equal share of all the prosperity that they enjoyed. The bias of national life has been so strong that neither geographical facts nor commercial tendencies have weakened the national bond. Nor are they more likely to do so now that Canada has, by the opening up of her great western provinces, manifestly entered upon a like period of development.

In spite of this evidence of a century's history Mr. Goldwin Smith still argues that trade interests will ultimately draw Canada into political connection with the United States, and apparently does not understand why his opinion is rejected with indignation by the vast majority of Canadians. Yet it seems impossible to conceive how, without a debasement of public sentiment quite unparalleled in history, a people whose history began in loyalty to British institutions, who through a hundred years have been sheltered by British power, who under that rule have attained and enjoyed the most complete political and religious liberty, who have constantly professed the most devoted regard for a mother land with which they are connected by a thousand ties of affectionate sympathy, should deliberately, in cold blood, and for commercial reasons only, break that connection and join themselves to a state in whose history and traditions they have no part. They would incur, and unquestionably would deserve, alike the contempt of the people they abandon and of the people they join. In a Great Britain reorganized as a federation, or union, or alliance, Canada would hold an honorable place, gained on lines of true national development; in annexation to the United States she could have nothing but a bastard nationality, the offspring of either meanness, selfishness, or fear.

George R. Parkin, *Imperial Federation The Problem of National Unity*, (London, Macmillan and Co., 1892), pp. 153-62.

The French-Canadian Question

Canada has had a two-fold history: French and English. The two elements of the population have not amalgamated to any appreciable extent, the hindrance arising from religion rather than race. We have then to-day a French-speaking Canada and an English-speaking Canada. It is important to keep in the mind a clear idea of the proportion of the one to the other. The tendency of the French population to remain concentrated in a single province or its immediate neighbourhood, (I do not forget the Acadian French, but they cannot seriously affect the position), makes it easy to indicate this proportion, and its fluctuation. In 1759 Quebec was Canada—a Canada entirely French and Roman Catholic. In 1791 Ontario was set off as a separate province, and within fifty years was of itself equal to the French province in population and superior in wealth. To-day Quebec is the only French-speaking province among the seven which make up the Confederation. An overflow into a few of the border counties of Ontario, a limited and scat-tered migration to the north-west, mark the only further expansion of the French population over new areas in Canada. A considerable migration to New England, where the Quebec peasant becomes a factory operative, is interesting, because it shows that he resists amalgamation in the United States as steadily as in Canada. Quebec, then, still represents French Canada. It has a population of 1,500,000, of whom 1,200,000 are French. It should be added that the wealth and influence of the great and growing city of Montreal are in the hands of the English minority, as were the wealth and influence of the city of Quebec in its days of greatest prosperity. A certain unprogressive spirit hampers the Frenchman, and gives a striking commercial and industrial advantage to the English population. Perhaps this contrast may in part be explained by the fact that the conquest of 1759 was followed by the return to France of a small, but intellectually and commercially important element of French Canadian society, while the English population was reinforced a few years later by an influx of loyalist energy and ability.

Roughly speaking, therefore, the French of Canada stand to the whole people as, at the most, a million and a half to five millions. The many provinces which are still to be carved out of the north-west will be English speaking. It is true that the French *habitants* have large families, and the natural increase of the race is somewhat greater than that of British colonists, but on the other hand the whole inflow of immigration increases the weight of the English-speaking provinces; the outflow to New England lessens that of Quebec. The relative influence and numbers of the French element in Canada will never be greater than they are at present, but rather less, partly owing, as

I have said, to the formation of new provinces, but even more to the hesitation of French Canadians to follow the advice of their wiser leaders like Mr. Laurier, and throw themselves more entirely than they have hitherto done into the tide of Anglo-Saxon movement on the continent. More than one historian has pointed out that the efforts of French kings and ministers to make Quebec a preserve for a single set of ideas paralyzed the energies of the colonists in early days. There seems to me to be a like danger now, arising from similar causes, that it may become the less energetic community of a strenuously progressive continent. But it can never dominate Canadian development, or permanently block the general movement of the Dominion in any given direction.

From another point of view French Canada to-day represents one of the most interesting triumphs of British constitutional government. When the Province of Quebec came under British dominion in 1763, it had never known what free government by the people meant. Governors and Intendants, with almost despotic power, or taking their orders even in minute detail from a French king or minister in Paris, left no room for popular control. Striking indeed was the contrast which the province presented to the English colonies further south, which from their very foundation began to organize a system of local self-government. In Quebec the beginnings of self-government had still to be made after 1763, or, rather, after 1774, the date of the Quebec Act. Yet the remark of Montalembert, that the Frenchman in Canada under British institutions has attained a liberty which the Frenchman of France never knew, is in strict accord with fact. France, which seems to have wasted few regrets on a colony which had always been poor

and a drain upon her resources, plunged into all the horrors of the Revolution to win a liberty which after all for more than a century has wavered between name and reality. The people of her surrendered colony, carrying on, along with the British provinces, the agitation for responsible government by methods entirely constitutional, save for the slight outbreak of 1837, have gained and continue in the secure enjoyment of a popular freedom as complete as that of any country in the world; a recognition for their religion such as that religion cannot command in France. Between the European Frenchman, moreover, and the French Canadian is the barrier raised by the Revolution. Modern France does not send emigrants to Quebec, where, indeed, they would scarcely be welcome. The typical French republican, with his atheism, his free life, and his contempt for religious forms, would be curiously out of place in the average French Canadian community, devout, moral, and conservative. He would, indeed, run no slight risk of being boycotted by clerical orders. The sentimental tie with France of race and language remains, and to the honour of French Canadians be it said, is fondly cherished, though it is not sustained by that constant intercourse and hearty literary sympathy which so bind the English world together. The reasoned political allegiance of the people goes out to the British connection, which gives steadiness to their public and security to their religious life.

Once more, French Canadians have profound objections to annexation to the United States. They go in numbers to work in the mills and factories of New England, or in the forests of Michigan or Maine for a few months or a few years, forming a large proportion of the so-called exodus, but those who become

naturalized American citizens have hitherto been an unimportant fraction of the whole. Many return, the movement to and fro being continuous. Those who stay form more or less distinct communities of their own, to which cohesion is given by the *curé*, who follows to supply the ministrations of their religion. The simple loyalty of the *habitant* to his Canadian home and to his religion is no slight offset to his narrowness of political outlook and his somewhat unprogressive habit of mind. It made him fight against American agression in 1774; it added a bright page to Canadian history by the heroic part taken in the war of 1812, when 400 French Canadians under de Salaberry defeated at Chateauguay an army of 3000 Americans. Happily we need not now think of like aggression, but should danger ever again threaten Canada, there are the strongest reasons to believe that the Frenchman even of the United States would soon find his place beside his compatriot in the old home, fighting for the land he loves with a passionate affection.

It is only natural that, with race, language, and religion on the one side, and on the other a heritage of free political institutions giving security to all of these, we should find fluctuations of expression among an excitable people in regard to national attachment. On the whole, however, the steadiness of French Canadian loyalty to British institutions is remarkable. . . .

. . . When a conspicuous French politician—not a Conservative—told me in Ottawa three years since that he would not be afraid to stand on any platform in Quebec and affirm that, in the event of war between France and England, other things being equal, four French Canadians out of every five would not only sympathize with, but prefer to fight for England, the energy of the statement was a surprise to me; but I have no reason to doubt the speaker's sincerity. The absolute truth of the statement cannot be questioned, if the supposed contest involved the substitution in Quebec of anti-religious French Republicanism, which the French Canadian hates, for the tolerant system of Britain. Looking back upon all that has happened in France since 1789, looking even at the condition of the Republic to-day and its attitude towards religion, the French Canadian may, and, it may be added, often does, sincerely echo the thought of the brilliant historian of the French occupation of America when he says that 'a happier calamity never befell a people than the conquest of Canada by the British arms.' . . .

It will be admitted that the experience of Sir John Macdonald in dealing with the French Canadian people, and his knowledge of French Canadian sentiment towards the Empire and the Dominion were unique. As a statesman he had every reason to consider and conciliate the French vote, by which his parliamentary majority was in part maintained throughout his career. Yet he never saw in French Canadian feeling any bar to a united Empire. In 1889, at a time when certain Quebec politicians, and even members of his own Cabinet, were declaiming rather vigorously against the idea of Imperial Federation, I had an opportunity of asking his opinion as to the ultimate attitude which Quebec was likely to take towards the question. His reply, given without reserve or hesitation, was marked by a decision which was manifestly the outcome of much thought upon the question. I try to reproduce this opinion, not so much to attach to it the weight of his great name, as because it bears upon the face of it the recommendation of

reason and truth. 'The relation of Quebec towards the Empire is fixed,' said he, 'by the facts of history and the aspirations of the people themselves. The controlling idea of the French Canadian is to retain his language, religion and civil institutions, necessarily held under a critical tenure on a continent in the main Anglo-Saxon. But he has in the treaty of 1763 and the Quebec Act founded upon it a Magna Charta as dear to him as is to an Englishman that won from King John. By that treaty the honour of England was pledged to France that the Frenchmen of Quebec who then became British subjects should be continued in the enjoyment of their religious and civil institutions. In annexation to the United States or in Canadian independence this guarantee would be given up. In the Great Republic the French Canadian would run the risk of being blotted out as was the Frenchman of Louisiana. In an independent Canada he would hold his own with difficulty. He must in the long run vote to follow the Empire in whatever direction its development may lead. This condition is permanent; all others are temporary. The interest of the French Canadian will lie in resisting separation, whether in the direction of independence or annexation.'

George R. Parkin, *Imperial Federation The Problem of National Unity*, (London, Macmillan and Co., 1892), pp. 46-49.

The White Man's Burden

To the Christian, the moralist, the philanthropist, no inspiration could be greater than that which might well spring from observing the growing strength of the Empire, and from reflection that this immense energy might be turned in directions which would make for the world's good. And strength beyond all other nations British people must have if they are to face in its fulness the work they have to do. . . . Three hundred millions of mankind, who do not share British blood, of various races and in various climes, acknowledge British sway, and look to it for guidance and protection; their hopes of civilzation and social elevation depending upon the justice with which it is exercised, while anarchy awaits them should that rule be removed. Through commerce and widespread territories the nation is brought into constant intercourse and often into the most delicate relations with almost every savage race on the globe, thus standing almost alone of European nations on that borderland where civilization confronts barbar-

ism, of all positions in which a nation can be placed perhaps the one most weighted with responsibilities and most pregnant with possibilities of good and evil. To this position the world's history offers no parallel; beside it Rome's range of influence sinks into comparative insignificance.

But to understand all that it means we must remember that along with this mighty growth of power there has been a steady growth of public conscience, which holds itself responsible not only for national acts, but for national influence; which refuses to shut its eyes to abuse of power, but rather looks upon power as a sacred trust, to be used for worthy ends. Therein lies the justification of our national greatness. . . .

. . . We have assumed vast responsibilities in the government of weak and alien races, responsibilities which cannot now be thrown off without a loss of national honour, and without infinite harm to those under our rule. A nation which has leaning upon it an Indian population of nearly 300,000,000 over and above the native races of Australasia, South Africa, and many minor regions, must require, if stability and equilibrium are to be maintained, an immense weight of that trained, intelligent, and conscientious citizenship which is the backbone of national strength. It needs to concentrate its moral as well as political strength for the work it has to do.

If we really have faith in our own social and Christian progress as a nation; if we believe that our race, on the whole, and in spite of many failures, can be trusted better than others, to use power with moderation, self-restraint, and a deep sense of moral responsibility; if we believe that the wide area of our possessions may be made a solid factor in the world's politics, which will always throw

the weight of its influence on the side of a righteous peace, then it cannot be inconsistent with devotion to all the highest interests of humanity to wish and strive for a consolidation of British power. It is because I believe that in all the noblest and truest among British people there is this strong faith in our national integrity, and in the greatness of the moral work our race has yet to do, that I anticipate that the whole weight of Christian and philanthropic sentiment will ultimately be thrown on the side of national unity, as opening up the widest possible career of usefulness for us in the future; inasmuch as it will give us the security which is necessary for working out our national purpose.

J. Castell Hopkins, "Canadian Hostility
to Annexation," *The Forum,* Vol. XVI
(Nov. 1893), pp. 325-35.

The Defects of American

Society

. . . In the United States . . . the
principle of "manifest destiny," as Charles
Sumner called it, runs like a thread
through every page of its international
history, and is woven into many parts of
its internal policy. The efforts made during the War of the Revolution to bring
the Canadian Provinces, or Colonies as
they were then called, into the new Confederation of States, are known to every
reader of history. In Article XI of the
Constitution of 1777 it was specially provided that

"Canada, acceding to the Confederation and
joining in the measures of the United States,
shall be admitted into, and entitled to all the
advantages of, this Union; but no other
Colony shall be admitted to the Union
unless such admission shall be agreed to by
nine States."

But the British provinces refused to be
won by persuasion and were left uncon-
quered by force. Most Canadians believe
to-day that the United States has shown a

steady, deliberate dislike of their country and has pursued a policy more or less
injurious to their interests.

The Oregon boundary dispute; the
Maine boundary troubles, settled, it was
thought, most unjustly by the Ashburton
Treaty; the San Juan question; the abro-
gation of the fishery clauses of the Washington Treaty; the Atlantic Coast fisheries
dispute; the refusal to allow Canadian
volunteers to cross American territory
during the North-West Rebellion and pre-
viously to the completion of the Canadian
Pacific Railway, although dozens of
American regiments had passed through
Canadian territory during the Civil War;
the annexation of Alaska in order, as Secretary Seward once pointed out, to prevent
British-Canadian extension on the Pacific
Coast and to strengthen American influence in British Columbia; the Bering Sea
fisheries dispute and the unfriendly manner in which Canadian sealers have been
treated; the McKinley bill and its injurious agricultural schedule; the Alien
Labor law, and its aggressive enforcement
against Canadians; the constant threats
regarding the Canadian Pacific Railroad;
and refusals to entertain any proposition
for fair reciprocity—all these things have
combined to make Canadians as a rule
consider the inhabitants of the Republic
what the Liberal Premier of Ontario
once termed them, "a hostile people."
And these historical incidents, these evidences of doubtful friendship, are among
the most powerful obstacles to future
union or closer relations.

Intimately connected with these considerations is the concealed dislike of so
many Americans to Great Britain or their
avowed hostility to its interests. Whether
this feeling is representative or not of the
United States as a nation, Canadians are
prone to look upon it in that light. . . . In

a word, another serious obstacle to annexation is the possibility, dim or vivid, as it may seem to the individual, that some day the United States may drift, or be dragged, into a war with Great Britain, which under Continental Union would force Canadians to be false to their new flag or else to the honor and gratitude which they owe to their mother-country. "Manifest destiny," therefore, is dependent for the first step towards realization upon the Canadian people's being impressed with a conviction of the genuine friendship entertained by the United States towards themselves and Great Britain. . . .

The defects in American national life have long been keenly studied and criticised in Canada, and the most enthusiastic advocate of annexation knows that this belief in the superiority of Canadian institutions, laws, politics and even morals, is ingrained in the heart of the average citizen whom he endeavors to convert. I will summarize briefly a few of the most important considerations which occur naturally to a Canadian when annexation is mentioned.

I. Responsible government, as compared with Presidential rule. In Canada the Governor-General represents the Queen and reigns but does not rule. Parliament sits, legally, for seven years—practically, for five or six years, and the Premier must have the confidence of its majority. If the country is generally alarmed or indignant, it acts upon the members and they vote against the Ministry. Public posts in the control of Parliament, or of its delegated representatives—the Ministry of the day—are held for life during good behavior. On the other hand, the United States has its President chosen in the midst of a violent turmoil every four years—every two years, if preparation be part of the battle

—and he is during his term responsible practically to nobody. The people cannot control him, Congress cannot overthrow his authority or that of his Cabinet, and the whole machinery of government, including the spoils system, rests to a great degree in the hands of one man.

II. Legislative methods. It is believed that injurious and poorly-digested laws, together with appropriations for large sums and important purposes, rushed through without care or consideration, are characteristic of the Congress system. These slipshod methods not only compel the courts to spend much time in testing the constitutionality of various laws, but encourage the corrupt legislation which is the chief source of lobbyism and its multitudinous evils. The absence from Congress of authoritative Cabinet spokesmen much enhances this difficulty, which has its root in that serious constitutional error, the lack of responsibility for legislation. At Ottawa, on the other hand, as in London, careful preparation is given by selected members of the Cabinet to all government bills, and where the measure is of vital import, the whole Cabinet probably deals with it clause by clause before submitting it to Parliament. After it is submitted to the House of Commons or to the Senate, as the case may be, all publicity is given to its terms. So with legislation on private bills, of which two months' notice is required and concerning which the fullest opportunity is given for criticism in the select committees to which the bills may be referred.

III. Divorce laws and morals. This consideration is alike important and difficult to deal with. It is not necessary to affect or presume superior national morality in order to express regret at the looseness of the marriage-tie in the great Republic. Cardinal Gibbons pointed out

not long ago that between 1867 and 1886 two hundred thousand divorces were granted in the United States, as compared with one hundred and sixteen given in Canada. The trouble, of course, is caused largely by a difference in the laws of the various States, which permit the anomalous and disgraceful condition of a man or woman's being married in one State and single in another. And Canadians are disposed to seeing in the vast number of divorces granted yearly in New York, Chicago and more Western centres, a reflection upon the morality of the community and an evidence of a widespread lack of respect for the sacredness of the marriage-tie. Whether justified or not, this feeling is almost universal in Canada and constitutes another considerable obstacle to closer national relationship.

IV. The elective judiciary. Canadians are exceedingly averse from any judicial system founded upon an electoral basis. They recognize the merits of the United States Supreme Court, the ability and impartiality which characterize its judges; but the respect paid to its decisions and to the Court itself is believed to be due to the fact that judges are carefully selected and hold office upon a life tenure. But lower down in the scale of courts, the unfortunate electoral system comes into play. At once, the lack of respect for the bench and its decisions we think, rightly or wrongly, becomes apparent; the judge is only an elected official, no longer impartial, but the servant of the people or of the party which elected him. In Canada, the judiciary is appointed for life and is composed of men of the highest legal standing. Sir John Macdonald, during his many years of Premiership, selected most of the principal judges, and, like the other party-leaders, chose men irrespective of their politics or political services. The consequence is that from the lowest court to the highest, the bench of Canada is admired and respected throughout the Dominion.

V. Lack of respect for law. Whether it be a result of the elective system or a consequence of innate lawlessness in a part of the population, the frequency of lynch-law outrages throughout the Union is to Canadians incomprehensible. The great Canadian North-West has been opened up, the Indians have been dealt with, a half-breed population has been trained in self-government, the mines of British Columbia have been made to produce fifty million dollars in gold, and that great province has been opened up to civilization and settlement, while thousands of miles of railway have been built, and all without one lynching! Such incidents, therefore, as the frightful tortures inflicted upon the negro who was burned to death at Paris, Texas; the hanging at Burnet, Texas, upon the very slightest suspicion, of a colored girl who was afterwards found to be innocent; the lynching of the man Denmark by a mob in South Carolina, with the Governor's practical connivance or approval, after the alleged victim had declared him innocent; these and similar occurrences produce a sensation of horror in the onlooker, equalled only by amazement as to the condition of the laws, or the public disregard of them, which permits such deeds. If they were exceptional and occasional, little would be thought of outbursts of this nature; but taking place constantly and extending as they do, from New Jersey to Texas, from New York to San Francisco, the average Canadian can hardly be blamed for disliking and fearing the general national conditions which permit such results.

VI. The spoils system. In Canada, positions in the Civil Service are obtainable after examination and are held during good behavior, which as a rule means for life. In the United States, the motto, "To the victors belong the spoils," has been lived up to in principle and practice. Senator Pendleton, during a speech on December 31, 1881, said that the idea that one hundred thousand offices, purely administrative, almost absolutely clerical in nature, paying one hundred million dollars a year in salaries, should be distributed by the President and his friends after every election, was a crime against civilization, and "the prolific parent of fraud, corruption and brutality." This is a severe indictment, but it represents a very general feeling in Canada, strengthened by such incidents as the contention of Mr. Blaine's friends that he was beaten at the Minneapolis Convention by office-holders; the many weeks' struggle of President Cleveland and his whole Cabinet with office-seekers, to the neglect of national business; and the recent discoveries of fraud in the Pension Bureau. . . .

It is unnecessary to go at length into other Canadian objections. The obstacle afforded by a tariff double or treble that of the Dominion, may be alleviated in time, if President Cleveland during his term of office is able to persuade Congress to lower the duties—presuming that he wishes to do so. The difficulty looming dark upon the horizon in connection with seven millions of negroes whom the average American is indisposed to treat upon equal terms; the extreme length to which monopolies and trusts are carried; the dislike felt to wealthy monopolists and the danger arising from the constant accumulation of huge fortunes in a few hands; the cost and turmoil of the almost continual elections; the memory of that near approach to civil war at the time of the Tilden-Hayes contest; the enormous expenditure upon pensions:—all these considerations militate against the spread of annexationism in Canada. Were the question to be publicly and generally discussed they would be heard of in every detail and particular from a thousand platforms—and this without anything but respect for the United States as a nation. . . .

. . . Canada is contented with her present national position, and conservative Canadians entertain a profound belief in the superiority of the British system of government over the American. They think the institutions, laws, morals, finance and legislation of the Dominion superior to those of the United States, and they would not care to risk serious changes through annexation. They are every year becoming more attached to Great Britain and more grateful for the power and liberty which can be obtained within the British realm. They are afraid of American aggression, suspicious of American dislike to the mother-land, averse from the necessity which would exist of hostile fiscal legislation under annexation, and of possible future conflict with Great Britain. They are becoming profoundly interested in the British market, as opposed to the old "sixty million market" theory, and have defeated by an overwhelming vote unrestricted reciprocity schemes which seemed to involve trade discrimination against England. Their commerce, railways, steamship lines, cable projects, and waterways all converge, east and west, toward Britain and British countries, instead of south to the United States. And of Americans who feel inclined to support passively or aid actively

some annexation propaganda, the majority of Canadians honestly ask, Why should you desire or expect us to do what you would never dream of doing yourselves? Why should Canada, with its vast and wealthy territory, its intimate connection with the greatest naval, commercial and territorial power on earth, and its splendid institutions, seek union with another nation, whatever its wealth and population, progress and prospects may be?

George T. Denison, "The Present Situation of England A Canadian Impression," *The Nineteenth Century,* Vol. 42 (Dec. 1897), pp. 1009-1018.

The Weaknesses of England

The events connected with the Jubilee in London this summer would lead the casual observer to the conclusion that the British Empire was world-wide in its extent, that it had planted its flag in every corner of the earth, that wherever its flag flew there were loyal subjects of Her Majesty, true to the common Empire, and ready to rally to its support and die for its safety. The Naval Review impressed one with the mighty sea-power of our Empire—in vessels, in men, in armament, in skilled officers, and in the warlike and national spirit that makes for national greatness. The Navy was never so strong and so efficient. No nation ever had such coaling stations, such fortified naval bases, so widely scattered and so well placed. One could not help feeling our great maritime strength.

The Colonial and Indian contingents impressed the imagination with the great reserve force, of the 11,000,000 Anglo-Saxon colonists and the hundreds of millions of other races, all giving their allegiance to the same Sovereign. . . . In fact, outwardly everything tended to prove that our Empire stood upon solid ground, prepared for all contingencies, and prosperous and progressive. . . .

The present temporary prosperity in England, which is not based upon a solid or permanent foundation, unfortunately tends still more to create the belief in the public mind that the state of affairs in England is satisfactory. I wish to draw attention to what seem to be the weak points in the present condition of the Mother Country. I had always been led to believe that the Free Trade policy of England was the secret of her success, and the foundation of her wealth and greatness. I was a Free Trader in Canada in 1878, and opposed the National policy at that time; and while I still believe that Free Trade was an advantageous policy for England at the time when Cobden and Bright advocated it, and that it has in the past added much to the prosperity and power of England by increasing immensely her trade and manufactures, yet I fear that experience has shown that there are weak points in the system, and that, like everything else, it has its faults as well as its advantages. If all nations had adopted the principle, as Cobden and Bright fully expected, it might have worked better; but free imports from foreign countries, and high taxes upon British exports into those countries, certainly cannot be called either 'Free' or 'Fair' Trade.

Protection in foreign countries has fostered and encouraged their own manufactures to such an extent as to reduce very much their imports of English goods, and to enable them to compete very successfully with the English trader, and cut down his trade as well as his profits. . . . At present England is living on her own fat, so to speak—the balances being made up by expenditures of capital, and

interest on the earnings and profits of years gone by.

The feature of the Free Trade policy that is most to be deplored is its effect on the great agricultural interests of England. The ill-effect is widespread, working evil in every direction. No one can travel through England without feeling sad at the evidences that crop up everywhere of the disastrous results threatened by this policy. The agricultural population is diminishing, the acreage under cultivation every year getting less, and the food-supply grown within the islands gradually trending towards the vanishing-point. Every year the population is drifting more and more into the manufacturing towns, increasing competition and making life harder to bear. Paupers are increasing in number every year, and the poor rates constantly going up. . . . In addition to this, a large majority of the children of England, instead of being reared in the open country, under the dome of heaven, are being huddled in crowded towns, under a pall of factory smoke, among the soot-begrimed walls of narrow courts and alleys paved with cinders, without a blade of grass or a green leaf to be seen. The foul air and crowding in ill-ventilated houses must be affecting the physique and stamina of the race, and the day will soon come, if it has not yet come, when England in defending her national existence will no longer be able to rely upon a great rural population of the type of those yeomen who drew the long-bow at Cressy, Poictiers, and Agincourt, or of those farmers' sons and village lads who in their solid squares hurled back the pride of France in our last great struggle at Waterloo. . . .

This, in my opinion, has been one outcome of the highly vaunted Free Trade policy—a huddling of the people into cities, a gradual weakening of the agricultural interest, a great decrease of country-bred men, and a decay in the size and stamina of the masses of the population. For a time England no doubt prospered pecuniarily, and great fortunes were made; but now, with imports almost double the exports, with the imports steadily increasing and the exports steadily diminishing, the nation is not even gaining in her manufactures, but is losing to other nations every day.

The design was to make England the workshop of the world; but why should that be the ambition of any nation? Why should the English be the serfs of the universe, and do the dirty work for mankind? . . .

The net result of fifty years of Free Trade on the one-sided principle has been to diminish the agricultural population and to weaken the physique of the British race, while even the chance of becoming the workshop of the world, which was the goal to be gained, is being lost. . . .

Above and beyond all the other evils I have mentioned is one which creates a great and pressing danger to our race, which should certainly be remedied at once in some way or other. The United Kingdom is dependent for its food on various sources of supply. The cultivation of wheat in England has decreased through foreign competition . . . and the sources of supply now are mainly confined to the United States and Russia, and countries under the control of Russia. . . .

To all outward appearance, the Jubilee taught the onlookers to believe that the British Empire was not only the wealthiest of all nations, but also the strongest at sea, and with an actual and reserve military strength equal to that of any nation; and that, with the strong feeling of loyalty that evidently actuated every

part, the Empire might defy the attacks of all comers. All this was apt to create an over-confidence in the public mind.

Of all the millions who witnessed the great pageants in June last, how very few considered the weak points!—the diminution in trade, the vanishing profits, the increasing foreign competition, and the destruction of the agricultural interest. How few considered the danger to England, and through her to the Empire, of the precarious and hand-to-mouth food supply! Every day that things go on as they are, we are in danger—a danger that is constantly becoming more threatening. Our Empire is leaving it in the power of two not over-friendly nations to combine, and, by putting an embargo upon all food products, to be able, possibly, to starve England into submission; and this they might do without capturing a gunboat, without winning a battle, without firing a shot. . . .

The Mother Country is today, as a nation, in the position, as it were, of an impregnable fortress, which has been armed with the finest artillery, supplied with munitions of war and military *matériel* without limit, garrisoned beyond its need, and stored with water for years, but in which no provision has been made for a secure supply of food, without which all the other precautions are absolutely useless. The great lesson to us all is that every effort should be made by all parts of the Empire to have this evil remedied, and the food supply made safe, in order that we may be self-dependent and self-sustaining in every particular. The food to feed the British people should be grown upon British soil, under the flag of the Empire, where it could be secured in case of war, and where it would be among people ready to fight for it and guard it for the common cause. . . .

The belief in the certainty of keeping command of the sea is also another instance of the feeling of over-confidence to which I have already alluded. I do not believe Great Britain can obtain the absolute and complete command of the sea everywhere. She may be able, and I hope and believe she will be able, to command certain routes and keep them open. She may be able to be in command, at any particular point where it is necessary for her to be in command, but it is unreasonable to expect that any fleet of 500 or even 700 ships could command all the sea routes, all the time, in all parts of the world. For this reason the food supply is the great and pressing danger, and should be put right at all hazards and at whatever cost may be necessary, either in money or theories.

There are several ways in which matters might be improved. National granaries is one suggestion, for which much can be said, and if adopted would make the Empire safer; but it would be a very costly method, and would be a greater burden in money than a duty on foreign corn, which might be imposed in place of the duty on tea, tobacco, and some other articles in common use by the people. Granaries, while adding to the safety, would add nothing to the wealth, progress, or stability of the Empire; but preferential tariffs would strengthen the Colonies immensely in population and wealth, would in the end strengthen and increase the trade of England, and would bind all parts of the Empire in the bonds of a common interest. If the preference was greater in favour of the home farmer, it would revive agriculture, and give employment to hundreds of thousands of men who are competing with the factory hands and tending to reduce wages. A sufficient duty, and it need not be large,

would ensure within the British Isles the growth of 15,000,000 quarters of wheat, instead of five or six millions as at present. [A] small preference of two or three shillings a quarter against the foreigner would increase the Canadian production by leaps and bounds. We have in Canada fertile wheat-bearing land, capable of producing the finest wheat in the world, in quantities far more than sufficient to feed Great Britain; and a slight preference would send emigration to fill up our fields and strengthen a portion of the Empire, instead of fostering and encouraging and building up foreign countries, which may at any time be hostile.

The sea route from Canada to England from the Straits of Belle Isle to the North of Ireland is almost a British route. It has no foreign naval stations to the North, and it is guarded by our stations at Halifax and St. John's on the West, and Portsmouth, Plymouth, Milford Haven and Bear Haven on the East. It is, without any doubt, the safest and most easily defended sea route from England in any direction.

The objection to this suggestion is that it would aid Canada. If it is not more important for England, and more advantageous to her ten times over than to Canada, it is not worth discussing; Canada is getting on all right. If her progress is not very fast, it is sure and on solid ground. We are not afraid of being starved into submission, and believe we can hold our freedom as a people, if it comes to straight fighting, as our fathers did in 1812, 1813, and 1814, against odds many times greater than we are likely to have to encounter now. But the British Empire is our Empire, as it is the Empire of every part; and we are as much interested in the safety of the heart of it as is any portion, and we have the right to urge that England shall take steps to make her condition safe.

If such a war should happen as we have been discussing, the heaviest brunt of the fighting would fall upon the Canadian people. Russia would probably attack India; and the United States, Canada. It is not a pleasant prospect for us to look forward to, with England's food supply in the condition it is. Six millions of us Northern men, fighting on our own soil for our homes and freedom and all we hold dear, would, we believe, be able to hold our own in spite of the odds; but in what a position would we be placed, if we heard of the men, women, and children of England starving and pleading for peace, and being told by the United States that we must lay down our arms before they would send the food to save the lives of our brethren in England!

We have a right to ask the English people to provide against this disaster, either by granaries, bounties, preferential tariffs, or in any other way. This should be done, not to carry out or to upset any trade theories, but as an insurance against a great national danger, as a necessary expenditure, as a war measure of defence.

Stephen Leacock, *Greater Canada An Appeal Let Us No Longer Be A Colony*, (Montreal, The Montreal News Company, 1907), pp. 1-10.

Imperialism as Anti-Colonialism

Now, in this month of April [1907], when the ice is leaving our rivers, the ministers of Canada take ship for this the fourth Colonial Conference at London. What do they go to do? Nay, rather what shall we bid them do? We—the six million people of Canada, unvoiced, untaxed, in the Empire, unheeded in the councils of the world,—we, the six million colonials sprawling our over-suckled infancy across a continent,—what shall be our message to the motherland? Shall we still whine of our poverty, still draw imaginary pictures of our thin herds shivering in the cold blasts of the North, their shepherds huddled for shelter in the log cabins of Montreal and Toronto? Shall we still beg the good people of England to bear yet a little longer, for the poor peasants of their colony, the burden and heat of the day? Shall our ministers rehearse this worn-out fiction of our 'acres of snow,' and so sail home again, still untaxed, to the smug approval of the oblique politicians of Ottawa? Or, shall we say to the people of England, "The time has come; we know and realize our country. We will be your colony no longer. Make us one with you in an Empire, Permanent and Indivisible."

This last alternative means what is commonly called Imperialism. It means a united system of defence, an imperial navy for whose support somehow or other the whole Empire shall properly contribute, and with it an imperial authority in whose power we all may share. To many people in Canada this imperialism is a tainted word. It is too much associated with a truckling subservience to English people and English ideas and the silly swagger of the hop-o'-my-thumb junior officer. But there is and must be for the true future of our country, a higher and more real imperialism than this—the imperialism of the plain man at the plough and the clerk in the counting house, the imperialism of any decent citizen that demands for this country its proper place in the councils of the Empire and in the destiny of the world. In this sense, imperialism means but the realization of a Greater Canada, the recognition of a wider citizenship.

I, that write these lines, am an Imperialist because I will not be a Colonial. This Colonial status is a worn-out, by-gone thing. The sense and feeling of it has become harmful to us. It limits the ideas, and circumscribes the patriotism of our people. It impairs the mental vigor and narrows the outlook of those that are reared and educated in our midst. The English boy reads of England's history and its glories as his own; it is *his* navy that fought at Camperdown and Trafalgar, *his* people that have held fast their twenty miles of sea eight hundred years against a continent. He learns at his fireside and at his school, among his elders and his contemporaries, to regard all this

as part of himself; something that he, as a fighting man, may one day uphold, something for which as a plain citizen he shall every day gladly pay, something for which in any capacity it may one day be his high privilege to die. How little of this in Canada! Our paltry policy teaches the Canadian boy to detach himself from the England of the past, to forget that Camperdown and Copenhagen and the Nile are ours as much as theirs, that this navy of the Empire is ours too, ours in its history of the past, ours in its safe-guard of the present.

If this be our policy and plan, let us complete our teaching to our children. Let us inscribe it upon the walls of our schools, let us write it in brass upon our temples that for the Navy which made us and which defends us, we pay not a single penny, we spare not a solitary man. Let us add to it, also, that the lesson may bear fruit, this "shelter theory" of Canada, now rampant in our day; that Canada, by some reason of its remoteness from European sin and its proximity to American republicanism, is sheltered from that flail of war with which God tribulates the other peoples of the world, sheltered by the Munroe Doctrine, by President Roosevelt and his battleships, sheltered, I know not how, but sheltered somehow so that we may forget the lean, eager patriotism and sacrifice of a people bred for war, and ply in peace the little craft of gain and greed. So grows and has grown the Canadian boy in his colonial status, dissociated from the history of the world, cut off from the larger patriotism, colourless in his ideas. So grows he till in some sly way his mind opens to the fence-rail politics of his country side, with its bribed elections and its crooked votes—not patriotism this, but 'politics,' maple-leaf politics, by which money may be made

and places and profit fall in a golden shower. . . .

. . . The time has come to be done with this *colonial* business, done with it once and forever. We cannot in Canada continue as we are. We must become something greater or something infinitely less. We can no longer be an appendage and outlying portion of something else. Canada, as a *colony,* was right enough in the days of good old Governor Simcoe, when your emigrant officer sat among the pine stumps of his Canadian clearing and reared his children in the fear of God and in the love of England—right enough then, wrong enough and destructive enough now. We cannot continue as we are. In the history of every nation, as of every man, there is no such thing as standing still. There is no pause upon the path of progress. There is no stagnation but the hush of death.

And for this progress, this forward movement, what is there first to do? How first unravel this vexed skein of our colonial and imperial relations? This, first of all. We must realize, and the people of England must realize, the inevitable greatness of Canada. This is not a vainglorious boast. This is no rhodomontade. It is simple fact. Here stand we, six million people, heirs to the greatest legacy in the history of mankind, owners of half a continent, trustees, under God Almighty, for the fertile solitudes of the west. A little people, few in numbers, say you? Ah, truly such a little people! Few as the people of the Greeks that blocked the mountain gates of Europe to the march of Asia, few as the men of Rome that built a power to dominate the world, nay, scarce more numerous than they in England whose beacons flamed along the cliffs a warning to the heavy galleons of Spain. Aye, such a little people, but growing,

growing, growing, with a march that shall make us ten millions tomorrow, twenty millions in our children's time and a hundred millions ere yet the century runs out. What say you to Fort Garry, a stockaded fort in your father's day, with its hundred thousand of today and its half a million souls of the tomorrow? What think you, little river Thames, of our great Ottawa that flings its foam eight hundred miles? What does it mean when science has moved us a little further yet, and the wheels of the world's work turn with electric force? What sort of asset do you think then our melting snow and the roaring river-flood of our Canadian spring shall be to us? What say you, little puffing steam-fed industry of England, to the industry of Coming Canada. Think you, you can heave your coal hard enough, sweating and grunting with your shovel to keep pace with the snow-fed cataracts of the north? Or look, were it but for double conviction, at the sheer extent and size of us. Throw aside, if you will, the vast districts of the frozen north, confiscate, if you like, Ungava still snow-covered and unknown, and let us talk of the Canada we know, south of the sixtieth parallel, south of your Shetland Islands, south of the Russian Petersburg and reaching southward thence to where the peach groves of Niagara bloom in the latitude of Northern Spain. And of all this take only our two new provinces, twin giants of the future, Alberta and Saskatchewan. Three decades ago this was the 'great lone land,' the frozen west, with its herds of bison and its Indian tepees, known to you only in the pictured desolation of its unending snow; now crossed and inter-crossed with railways, settled 400 miles from the American frontier, and sending north and south the packets of its daily papers from its two provincial capitals. And of this country, fertile as the corn plains of Hungary, and the crowded flats of Belgium, do you know the size? It is this. Put together the whole German Empire, the republic of France and your England and Scotland, and you shall find place for them in our two new provinces. Or take together across the boundary from us, the States of Maine, New Hampshire, Vermont, Massachusetts, Rhode Island and Connecticut,—all the New England States —and with them all the Middle States of the North—New York, New Jersey, Pennsylvania, Delaware, Ohio, Indiana, Michigan, Illinois and Wisconsin,—till you have marked a space upon the map from the Atlantic to the Mississippi and from the Ohio to the lakes—all these you shall put into our two new provinces and still find place for England and for Scotland in their boundaries.

This then for the size and richness of our country. Would that the soul and spirit of its people were commensurate with its greatness. For here as yet we fail. Our politics, our public life and thought, rise not to the level of our opportunity. The mud-bespattered politicians of the trade, the party men and party managers, give us in place of patriotic statecraft the sordid traffic of a tolerated jobbery. For bread, a stone. Harsh is the cackle of the little turkey-cocks of Ottawa, fighting the while as they feather their mean nest of sticks and mud, high on their river bluff. Loud sings the little Man of the Province, crying his petty Gospel of Provincial Rights, grudging the gift of power, till the cry spreads and town hates town and every hamlet of the country-side shouts for its share of plunder and of pelf. This is the tenor of our politics, carrying as its undertone the voice of the black-robed sectary, with narrow face and shifting eyes, snarling still with the bigotry of a by-

gone day. This is the spirit that we must purge. This is the demon we must exorcise; this the disease, the canker-worm of corruption, bred in the indolent security of peace, that must be burned from us in the pure fire of an Imperial patriotism that is no theory but a passion. This is our need, our supreme need of the Empire—not for its ships and guns, but for the greatness of it, the soul of it, aye for the very danger of it.

Of our spirit, then, it is not well. Nor is it well with the spirit of those in England in their thoughts of us. . . . Can they not see, these people of England, that the supreme English Question now is the question of Canada? that this Conference of the year of grace 1907 might, if it would, make for us the future of the Empire? Or will they still regard us, poor outlying sheltered people of Canada, as something alien and apart, sending us ever of their youngest and silliest to prate in easy arrogance of 'home,' earning the livelihood their island cannot give, still snapping at the hand that feeds them?

And what then can this Colonial Conference effect, after all, it is asked? . . . if we pay for this our Navy that even now defends us, and yet speak not in the councils at Westminster, then is that Taxation without Representation . . .[?]

So there we stand, we and you, pitched fast upon the horns of a dilemma. You cannot tax us, since you will not represent us. We cannot be represented because we will not be taxed. . . .

Yet is the difficulty perhaps not impossible of solution. The thing to be achieved is there. The task is yours to solve, men of the council table. . . .

Nor is guidance altogether lacking in the task. For at least the signs of the times are written large as to what the destiny of Canada shall *not* be. Not as it

is,—not on this *colonial* footing,—can it indefinitely last. There are those who tell us that it is best to leave well alone, to wait for the slow growth, the evolution of things. For herein lies the darling thought of the wisdom of the nineteenth century, in this same Evolution, this ready-made explanation of all things; hauled over from the researches of the botanist to meet the lack of thought of the philosopher. Whatever is, is: whatever will be, will be,—so runs its silly creed. Therefore let everything be, that is: and all that shall be, shall be! This is but the wisdom of the fool, wise after the fact. For the solution of our vexed colonial problem this profits nothing. We cannot sit passive to watch our growth. Good or bad, straight or crooked, we must make our fate.

Nor is it ever possible or desirable that we in Canada can form an independent country. The little cry that here and there goes up among us is but the symptom of an aspiring discontent, that will not let our people longer be colonials. 'Tis but a cry forced out by what a wise man has called the growing pains of a nation's progress. Independent, we could not survive a decade. Those of us who know our country realize that beneath its surface smoulder still the embers of racial feud and of religious bitterness. Twice in our generation has the sudden alarm of conflict broken upon the quiet of our prosperity with the sound of a fire-bell in the night. Not thus our path. Let us compose the feud and still the strife of races, not in the artificial partnership of an Independent Canada, but in the joint greatness of a common destiny.

Nor does our future lie in Union with those that dwell to the Southward. The day of annexation to the United States is passed. . . .

Not Independence then, not annexation, not stagnation: nor yet that doctrine of a little Canada that some conceive,—half in, half out of the Empire, with a mimic navy of its own; a pretty navy this, —poor two-penny collection, frollicking on its little way strictly within the Gulf of St. Lawrence, a sort of silly adjunct to the navy of the Empire, semi-detached, the better to be smashed at will. As well a Navy of the Province, or the Parish, home-made for use at home, docked every Saturday in Lake Nipigon!

Yet this you say, you of the Provincial Rights, you Little Canada Man, is all we can afford!—we that have raised our public charge from forty up to eighty millions odd, within the ten years past, and scarce have felt the added strain of it. Nay, on the question of the cost, good gentlemen of the council, spare it not. Measure not the price. It is not a commercial benefit we buy. We are buying back our honour as Imperial Citizens. For, look you, this protection of our lives and coast, this safe-guard from the scourge of war, we have it now as much as you of England: you from the hard-earned money that you pay, we as the peasant pensioners of your Imperial Bounty.

Thus stands the case. Thus stands the question of the future of Canada. Find for us something other than mere colonial stagnation, something sounder than independence nobler than annexation, greater in purpose than a Little Canada. Find us a way. Build us a plan, that shall make us, in hope at least, an Empire Permanent and Indivisible.

Arnold Winterbotham, ed., *Canadian Addresses by the Hon. George Foster,* (Toronto, Bell & Cockburn, 1914), pp. 134-43, 146-47, 149-60, 162-63, 167-77.

"Naval Defence". 'Speech delivered in the House of Commons, Ottawa, March 29, 1909, on the motion: "That in the opinion of this House, in view of her great and varied resources, of her geographical position and national environments, and of that spirit of self-help and self-respect which alone befits a strong and growing people, Canada should no longer delay in assuming her proper share of the responsibility and financial burden incident to the suitable protection of her exposed coast-line and great seaports".'

Naval Defence

For a good many years I have been more and more impressed with the necessity of our facing the question involved in this resolution. Nothing particular has been done with it so far in parliament. I do not think that we mitigate any difficulties by avoiding them, or get rid of any of our responsibilities by evading them, and it seems to me that the time has now come when the parliament and people of Canada should sit down together and take stock of the situation and come to some conclusion as to whether they have duties, and what these duties are, regarding the great question of the defence of our common heritage.

Now we have all sympathy with that class of good and estimable men who declare that war is horrible, that its burdens are almost intolerable, and that its effects are wide reaching and in the main injurious, and who, in our country as in others, declare that we want no armaments, no militarism, no defences, that ours is an era of peace, and that we should strive, as best we can, to make this good in principle and in action, without arbitrament of war. But whilst I have sympathy with this view, I have taken into account the history of the world and the lesson it teaches. And whether I be right or wrong, I draw from the history and experience of the world this one great fact—that force, absolute physical force, lies at the foundation of all our progress and civilization.

In the primeval times physical force expressed itself and exposed itself in bare and brutal form. To-day it is surrounded with and disguised by the trappings and refinements of civilization; but in the last resort it is there. Just as underneath the varied soils, beautiful in varied growth, there yet lies the solid granite-base, the foundation and guarantee of permanence, so under all the civilization and refinement of to-day there is to be found, in the last analysis, the appeal to physical force. A man meets his neighbour as individual against individual. If he can persuade him by argument, if he can prevent and restrain him by quoting the law and the conventions of society, well and good; but if none of these prevail, it is his right and duty to defend himself by sheer physical force. In the family, the school, the city, the province, the country, the situation, in the last analysis, is similar. If there are mischievous members of society, who are not amenable to Christian teachings or to moral ethics, then the force of the law

has to deal with them, and the constable, the policeman, the militia, and the standing army, if need be, are resorted to as the personification of a physical force that is conclusive.

If this is true of society and the individual, it is equally true with reference to nations. From the earliest times to the present there have been mischievous, unscrupulous, and ambitious peoples who have compelled resort in the end to physical force. We deduce therefore this fact that to defend and to preserve is the right and the duty of the individual, of society, and of the nation, and that if it is necessary to do this by force, then force must be invoked. The right and duty of the individual is the right and duty of the aggregation of individuals, that is of the nation itself. As we find the selfish and the unscrupulous and the strong preying upon society, so among nations it has always been, so it is now, and so, as far as I can see, it will be for our own lives, and very probably for many generations thereafter. *In fact, the more inviting the situation that a country possesses, if it is combined with weakness and lack of preparation, the more that country becomes the prey and the mark of the ambitious, of the unscrupulous, of the strong.*

There are considerations which act as restraints: the jealousies of surrounding nations, the *ententes cordiales*, the pacts, the agreements, the commercial ties, the world's conscience—all these restrain and retard and moderate. But some day all these become storm-swept, and the naked sword flashes out in defence of altar and hearth-fires. All history teaches the lesson of this insecurity and that the nation which is forewarned and forearmed, which makes its preparation with proper care, is the only nation that has reasonable security and guarantee of existence.

Consider the last fifty years of the greatest and most civilized century of the world, and what are the examples? The fire that was kindled on the Crimea, the blood-red streams that ran in India, the long struggle in the United States between the South and North, the Franco-Prussian war, the Spanish-American battles, the British-Boer war, and the Japan-Russian war—all these are outstanding, large examples of the fact that all the restraints of Christian morals and of ethics are impotent to curb the ambitions and the passions of nations; examples of the sad disappointments of those who believed that the era of peace, and enduring peace, had been at last ushered into existence. *Today we must come to the conclusion that neither Christian teaching nor peace conventions, nor strong commercial liens, nor Hague conferences, nor Triple Alliances, nor Berlin Treaties, can guarantee peace.* In a single night, within the last few weeks, a great nationality tore in tatters the Treaty of Berlin, and the lurid war-cloud hovered over the Balkans and shot its lightnings into every chancellory in Europe, and even to-day the unrest is not stilled.

Into this world of trouble, of uncertainty, amongst this world of nations, Canada has pushed forward to her place. She has taken a position which is important now, which will become more and more important as the years advance. Her ship of state is launched on the world's waters, it is open to every storm, it is exposed to every danger. *She cannot escape the common burden, she cannot neglect the common duty, she cannot ignore the common responsibility.* I do not believe that she wishes to. Having entered the game, I believe that it is the disposition of the Canadian people to play it valiantly, to play it honourably, and to play it suc-

cessfully. If her sons have the pride of manhood, as I believe they have, if they know what the stern joy of contest means, if they have proper faith in their high destiny, if they visualize any adequate picture of the future, it seems to me it is for the people of Canada and for the manhood of Canada to prove their faith and their worth by their works, to grasp the full meaning of their heritage and its responsibilities, and to prepare to defend it as well as to develop it.

And what has Canada to defend? Her vast national resources, ever unfolding, inestimable in quantity and of excellent quality, but more significant in one sense, in the particular time at which in God's good province she has commenced to enter into their development, the time in the history of the world's advancement in which she has commenced to exploit, in this last great west, what is to be of such worth, of such value and of such resource to the whole world. She has her extended coast-line, her ports, her harbours, with coal supplies at the pit's mouth almost open to the bunkers of the vessels, her immense resources of food supply, her rivers and her lakes stretching through the centre of her vast country. East and west, across two mighty oceans, she is face to face with two immense masses of human activity—on one side, in the Orient, 350,000,000 people waking up into a new life, an activity the outcome of which no man at present living can define; on the other side, the activities of the old and well-known nations of Europe. On the south she is face to face with the most compact and powerful people on the globe, and in the background, the wide cool reaches of the north, silent and mysterious. . . .

*Observe her lines of communication and transport, built by her own people, aided with money from foreign countries, but mainly from Britain. Look at the development of her transportation system; whether directed by policy, whether by providence, or whether it was what we may call the compulsion of circumstances, there it lies. Mark all the great lines of railway transport east and west, moving from the central zones towards the ocean on the west, or to the ocean on the east; her rivers flowing east and west, and the great lakes which empty therein, river and lake passing close to the homes of the farmer and the marts of our people, stopping by the side of her wharfs and her docks, and saying: "Here I am ready to work; load me up with your treasures, and I will bear them to the sea." Along the lines of railway transport and the great lines of natural transport by lake or river we are everywhere seeking the seaport for embarkation, everywhere bound outward on the pathway of the sea to oversea ports and outside markets; and the one absolute condition of prosperity and permanency is that the ports of embarkation and the seapath to the ports of ultimate destination must be secure. That is the essential thing. . . .

As to naval defence, what have we done? I think we might just as well be frank with ourselves and say we have done nothing. From the earliest dawn of history, commerce and the protection of commerce have gone hand in hand. They have sailed the seas together, and worked out their beneficent purpose of development and protection side by side. You cannot point in history to a single commercial people that neglected to provide a protection more or less adequate for their commerce. We are a people nearly a century old, with the mighty heritage of which I have spoken, a heritage which is not simply for our own enjoyment but

which is to be transmitted to the generations—the far distant generations—that
succeed us. We to-day, in parliament and
in the country, have to acknowledge to
each other, if we will be frank, that we
have done no single effective thing in the
way of naval defence. . . .

In the meantime, whilst we have been
doing nothing, Cape Colony, a comparatively poor colony and sparsely populated,
has made a contribution of £50,000
annually; Natal, a small and comparatively poor colony and of sparse population,
has made its contribution of £35,000
annually; New Zealand has given
£40,000 annually, now increased to
£100,000, and Australia £200,000,
altogether a contribution of a million and
three-quarters of dollars per year, whilst
the British taxpayer goes down in his
pocket for £34,000,000—$3.60 per unit
—to maintain the naval defence of the
Empire. When we read these names,
Natal, Cape Colony, New Zealand, and
Australia, the name of Canada does not
appear, and as we look at that procession
in the first line of defence we come to the
conclusion, and it is not an exhilarating
one, that not only have we not put a
dollar into the naval defence of Canada
for her own coasts, but that not a ship in
the procession bears the name of Canada
and that not a stiver or a sixpence of the
mighty expense of that great battle line
has been contributed out of the money of
Canada. This grips our attention. It gives
us at least, to press it no further, reason
for thought. To some, and I confess to
myself, it appears necessary for very
shame's sake that we do something and
do something adequate.

"But," says some objector, "Great
Britain is bound to protect the Empire;
her prestige demands it, her necessities
demand it." That argument is not the
argument of the brave, or of the generous-
hearted, or of the self-respecting, or of
the properly independent man, and it is
not the argument for a young and growing people which is a candidate for admission amongst the nations of the
earth. . . .

To-day Great Britain has her armed
guards on the Pamirs and in the passes
of the Himalayas, her sentinels on every
frontier line, her sailors and flag in every
sea, her bodies of living scarlet and khaki
here and there dispersed throughout the
world; and though she has done all that
and bears the immense burden to-day, she
has yet to exact the first penny of tribute
from any country that she has liberated
or any people that she has made free.
Every dollar of the money, every drop of
the blood worth more than money, poured
out so lavishly and so long in those great
world efforts, has been contributed by the
people of the British Isles. For five centuries the patient, toiling British taxpayer
has paid the bill and paid it with a cheer-
ful countenance, and without grumbling.
Can you find in the history of the world
any more sublime figure and any more
beneficent instrumentality for good worked in so unselfish a way and borne so
cheerfully and unstintingly by the few
millions of people that live in the islands
in the North Sea? What rank ingratitude
in us, of all people, to shield our selfish
indifference to the sacrifices of such a
mother behind such an argument.

Some may say: "We are safe in
Canada, the Monroe doctrine will be all
that we need, the United States will not
allow any foreign country to plant its flag
on the soil of the North American continent; we are immune, because of the
Monroe doctrine." The Monroe doctrine
and the United States of America might
guarantee our safety from foreign inva-

sion, but what would be the price that Canada would have to pay? The humiliation of it would be like the Cain's mark on the brow of every Canadian; the degradation of it would eat into the heart of every man until he grew servile and cringing. The price we should have to pay would be continual demand, continual concession, until at last absorption finished the craven course, covered up our name and blotted out our hope of a national future. Bad enough for us to hang on to the apron strings of a loving, opulent mother, but when we have grown to manhood it is the negation of every principle of manhood and independence that we should live in our national home by the grace of the stranger, however well intentioned and kind he might be. I put away the Monroe doctrine as absolutely unthinkable for us as a shelter under which to grow up to national manhood. I come then to the conclusion, imperfectly argued out, I know: That protection is necessary, absolutely necessary; that we cannot as a people owe our protection to the United States of America, or to any other foreign power; that that protection must either be borne by ourselves or by ourselves in conjunction with Great Britain and in co-operation with the Mother Country.

I propose shortly to take up the question of how this protection is to be given. . . .

The first is the policy of a fixed annual contribution in money to the British Government or the British Admiralty. . . . We are not in a position to build and equip and send over Dreadnoughts. When we translate our contribution into Dreadnoughts it comes down in the end to money which would be sufficient to build and equip a Dreadnought, and therefore I say they are both parts of

the one proposition, an annual fixed contribution of money to the British Government for the purpose of national and imperial defence; or, if you would rather have it, for the purpose of Canada's defence through imperial co-operation and imperial supreme command in war times.

The first difficulty in that is as to fixing the amount of the contribution. . . .

Another objection raised is that it smacks too much of tribute, that we are a free people, and we do not want to be paying a contribution to the old country for this or for any other purpose. I do not take much stock in that objection. Not one atom of our autonomy, not one atom of our independence, not one atom of our power as a parliament is taken away from us because we decide and by vote do place a certain sum of money into the hands of the British Government or the British Admiralty to be applied to the purpose of our, and the Empire's, defence. It is not demanded of us; there is no tribute unless there is force, and unless there is a specific demand which brings the tribute. A fixed sum may be a most willing gift of the most liberty-enjoying legislature in the world.

We pay, someone will object, but we do not control. That is true; but what are we paying for? We are paying for a portion of the defence of the Empire, including ourselves. If we believe that the British Government and the British Admiralty have the widest experience, the greatest knowledge, the plans of war more thorough, the expert skill, every appliance and every accompaniment of the effective use of the money which we give, does it matter after all so very much whether we follow the course of the expenditure of that money or not? So that I do not take too great stock in that objection.

Another objection that is made is

that Britain may use our contribution in unjustifiable wars, and that we should guard ourselves carefully lest we make a contribution for the equipment and strengthening of a fleet which may be used in wars that we do not approve of. That might be with some countries an objection; but if you take the history of Great Britain for the last fifty years or more you may pretty fairly come to the conclusion that, as she has not and is not now, so in the future Great Britain will not be liable to carry on unjustifiable wars of conquest. . . . The whole spirit of the old country and its history for the last half-century may make us pretty sure that wars of conquest, undertaken for aggressive purposes and for mere lust of battle, are not likely to take place so far as Great Britain is concerned.

While these objections have some force, though as I think not a force that is irresistible, there are some reasons which appear to me to have deeper significance with reference to that method of taking our part in defence.

The first and greatest objection which I have to a fixed money contribution is that it bears the aspect of hiring somebody else to do what we ourselves ought to do; . . .

It goes still further than that. Suppose we contribute this year our sum, and next year our equal sum, and therafter year after year. After ten or twelve or twenty or thirty years we shall have paid out an immense amount of money. We shall have been protected in the meantime; but in Canada itself there will be no roots struck, there will be no residue left, there will be no preparation of the soil, or beginning of the growth of the product of defence. Yet some time or other, no one can doubt that, with resources and with a population constantly increasing,

we must and shall have in this country a naval force of our own for our coast and home defence. . . .

The second line to which I would refer is the assumption by ourselves of the defence of our own ports and coasts, in constant and free co-operation with the imperial forces of the Mother Country. . . .

Under that system our first vessels would be British built, British equipped, British manned, and British officered from stoker to captain. There is no other way in which we could proceed. We are absolutely bare of the skill, the experience, the training, and the machinery necessary to put one single war vessel on a proper footing; but—and it is but the beginning of a circle—the first Canadian owned vessel, built and equipped in Britain, and sent out to defend our coasts, would become the nucleus and the training ground of Canadian stokers, Canadian sailors, and Canadian officers, and by and by, perhaps, of a Canadian admiral on the Canadian coast. How much time would be taken in completing that circle none of us can say, but if we begin the tracing of it and follow it fairly and faithfully, the time must come when we get a complete circle and have an imperial adjunct to the British navy for the defence of Canada and the defence of the Empire, in which Canada has some of her body, her bones, her blood, and her mental power, her national pride. . . .

Cannot we trust the Mother Country? She has done enough for us in the past and showed her good-will. Are we afraid of losing our autonomy? Every move of Great Britain has been to shift responsibility upon us rather than to take it from us. What has she denied to us? If she has erred in any way it has been in the sentiment now wholly extinct that the colonies had better go and fend for them-

selves; but to-day no man can point a finger to a policy or a solid weighty utterance of Great Britain in which there is the least shadow of a proof that she even harbours the faintest idea of depriving one of the overseas dominions of her perfect autonomy. . . .

I do not know which of these forms our aid will take after due care and consideration, but, whichever form is chosen, one thing is certain, that something ought to be done—and done now. Our circumstances, our manhood, our sense of gratitude and our sense of right all demand that something should be done, something adequate, and something now. . . .

For what have we had from Great Britain? Our heritage—we are proud of it and we boast of it—has been conquered and held against all comers by Great Britain. . . .

Thereafter by her army and navy she has guaranteed our security. Our eastern gateway stands open, our western gateways are unblocked, the ocean path is as secure as the streets of a city. Why? Because of the guarantee of Britain's navy and of Britain's prestige. For all of that she has not asked one penny of tribute from these people, she has placed no contribution upon them. Our borders have been preserved. When the Fenian Raids of 1866 took place, what was the power that stood upon our frontier? The British regulars joined with our own volunteers stood as the defence of Canada. The British Government paid all the bills; and the British Government afterwards paid the indemnity for the damages which were caused by the invaders. When the Red River rebellion took place and our western heritage was in danger, it was Wolseley and the British regulars who, with our own volunteers, made the long and tedious journey to that distant section,

and stood for the protection of our nascent nationality. Great Britain paid all the bills. In the Riel rebellion our volunteers and our resources were sufficient to quell the rising; but just outside the ring stood the might and power of Britain, ready to interfere if anyone had lifted hand against the nationality and the integrity of this country.

Our rights have been upheld, our rights of fishery and navigation in the Atlantic and on the Pacific. When the threat was made that if Canadian vessels were found within the prescribed sealing area they would be confiscated, and our men imprisoned, it was the might of Britain which intervened and saved Canadians from arrest and indignity. . . .

Our liberties have been guarded. What have we asked that has not been given to us? Much that we have not asked has been freely bestowed. The rivals in long years of war, when once the war was ended, became equals in peace, guaranteed in their language, their creed, their rights and their privileges; and from that day to this we have lived together in peace, joined as Canadian citizens in common love for our common country, and a desire to develop it and to make it, if we can, the greatest in the world.

Our commerce has been protected. Wherever a Canadian vessel goes, wherever a Canadian trader travels, there he finds in every city, in every port, the ubiquitous protection of the fleet, and he finds there a representative of the best consular and diplomatic service in the world. All of these things cost money, all these are maintained there by Britain. The expense of every diplomatic establishment and of every consular agency is paid for by the British Government and is at our free service. . . .

All these we have accepted, on all

these we have relied, by all these we have profited, and the only thing we have given in return is now and then some cheap criticism, and more or less scant gratitude—not a very worthy return for the services that have been given to us. If we had been dependent on ourselves, what harassing, overshadowing fears would have been ours? To what perils should we have been exposed by sea and by land? What tremendous expenses should we have incurred with insufficient national insurance? What greater disaster might we not have suffered, extending even to loss of home, of name, of distinctive national existence? That for a century our farmers have tilled their acres in perfect peace; that in peace our fishermen have gathered their waterbred harvests, the merchant handled his wares, the doors of external commerce been kept continually open and the ocean passage-ways secured from molestation, is due to the fact that we have been safely insured in the greatest guarantee company of the ages, John Bull and Company, who has charged us no annual premiums, who has given us an incontestable policy, and a security unquestionable, so far as anything can be unquestioned in this variable world of ours.

But Britain has also been our banker. Her money has built, or partly built, our great railways, our canals, many even of our public buildings. Her money has furnished the lifeblood for our municipalities, for our great corporations, for our great industrial concerns and development companies. To what nation amongst all the nations could we have gone with such assets, and received such assurances of good-will, of ready resources and low rates of interest? . . .

Someone, perhaps, wearied by all this, will say: "Well, let Great Britain fight her own battles, she is able to do it." Certainly she is. But suppose her battles are our battles, how then should we look at it? Her battles have been our battles, her battles of the future will be battles for her defence and the defence of those that belong to her as dependent and overseas dominions. I cannot conceive, as I said before, of Britain fighting an aggressive war. To-day she is not an aggressor, she has not been for half a century. Her wars are our wars, her battles are our battles. One sees plainly, if a fleet were to invade this country and the British fleet were to range itself against our enemies off our own coasts, that it would be our battle waged in our defence. But suppose the battle be fought off the coasts of the threatening enemy; suppose, better yet, it be fought in the emergent pass ways when the vessels of the enemy are issuing from their ports one by one in straggling order before their full fighting power is possible and their full deployments made, is not that our battle just the same as if it were fought within sight of our own coasts? It seems to me that the best place to fight a battle for the defence of Canada, for the defence of Australia, is to fight it in the very ports and passage-ways of the enemy. That is the first, the primal, the effective line of defence. We must not think that because we are not within sound of the artillery, or in sight of the vessels that are engaged therein, it is therefore not our battle.

William L. Grant, "The Fallacy of Nationalism," *Empire Club Addresses Delivered to the Members During the Session of 1911-12*, (Toronto, 1913), pp. 223-228. Reprinted by permission of the Empire Club.

The Impossibility of

Isolationism

This question of Nationalism is in the modern sense rather a new thing. Territorial sovereignty, dynasty, empire, state —all these are very old things; but a nation, in the sense of a people with coherent boundaries awakening to a common consciousness really took its rise only after the French Revolution.

As long as the armies of France had only the monarchs to contend with, they swept resistlessly across Europe and brought in their train many of the blessings of civil and religious liberty. It was only when they had aroused the national spirit of Spain, Germany, Austria, and greatest of all, of England, it was only when they had not merely the monarchs to contend with but the nations in alliance with the monarchs, that Napoleon was overthrown.

At the Congress of Vienna, which closed the great Napoleonic struggle, the diplomats—always the class of men most inaccessible to new ideas,—tried to confine the new stream of life within the old

bounds, and much of the history of the nineteenth century consists of the struggle of the nations to win the unity which diplomacy had denied them. In its best known examples, Germay and Italy, it was a struggle for a larger unity. These countries had been left in 1815 mere geographic expressions. So recent and so remarkable is the present German unity that many of us forget that within the lifetime of men not yet old, the States of the present German Empire were engaged in bitter internecine strife. On this side then we have the struggle for larger unity; but there was also the side of dismemberment; the tearing away of Belgium from Holland was, as is the desire of Hungary for separation from Austria, a struggle for complete independence which too often degenerated into mere tribalism.

All these nationalistic strivings in Europe were based on the desire for self-sufficiency, the desire to move uninterrupted in the national orbit. Now, in this there was much that is good, much that is splendid; it meant that the people who were striving were willing to confront the ultimate issues of life and death, to give the last full measure of devotion; it was a spirit which hardened the fibre and turned gristle into bone.

In that sense Nationalism would do us in Canada no little good. There is widely spread in Canada a vague feeling that if anything turns up we shall be protected by a curious combination of the Monroe doctrine and the British navy. I object, in that sense at least, to the word protection. When I lived in England, one heard of a certain type of ladies who lived in some parts of London under the protection of certain gentlemen. Theirs was a profession considered to be more lucrative than honourable, and I have no desire that this country of mine should be either

the kept woman of the United States, or the harlot of the Empire.

Seeing the good which this Nationalism did and how strongly it made the red blood flow through the veins, certain political thinkers have felt that in Nationalism the last word has been spoken and have upheld it as the final goal of political effort. They have felt that the ideal for the British Empire was to be divided off into a number of small independent unities, Canada, Australia, New Zealand, South Africa, Egypt, India, England, Scotland, Ireland, Wales—each working out its own little destiny, each giving its picturesque little part to the great world process. They went back to ancient history and pointed out that the little city states of Greece were much more interesting than the great empires of Macedonia and Rome, which trampled out the individual and the picturesque, as beneath the great damp foot of a hippopotamus.

And yet in this idea there lies a fallacy, and the fallacy is the belief that in this modern world there is any such thing as independence. In this new world, every state is bound to every other state by filaments as impalpable yet as real and as numerous as those which thrill the instruments of Marconi. You cannot touch any part of the net-work without sending a thrill through every other part. Agadir is an unimportant harbour in the most savage portion of a semi-barbarous state, still so unknown that a week ago a candidate for the civil service examination told me that it was a city in the interior of Egypt; yet in July last an obsolescent German gunboat paid a peaceful visit to this unknown harbour, and Europe found herself on the verge of Armageddon. . . .

This suggests that vortex of militarism from which we would fain be free. The only answer is that to be free is quite impossible; that, as Sir Hibbert Tupper said, we are already in it up to the neck. We are only at the beginning of Canada; we have only got 8,000,000 people; yet we have already had a tariff war with Germany, and we have big commitments in Mexico and South America; only last night we found out that we had preferential trade with the West Indies; we have made a direct treaty with France; and yet we say we can be independent. . . .

On the west we look out towards Japan and the awakened Orient; on the other side to the nations of Europe; on the south we have the United States. I deny entirely the theory that the United States are to be our enemies, hereditary or otherwise. It is part of the high destiny of Canada to bring to perfection the unity of Great Britain and the United States. But in our dealings with the United States we must show a little knowledge of national psychology, a knowledge which, in their dealings with us, the United States have not always shown. The United States will not be friendly with a country if it does not preserve its self-respect; the great Republic is not a nation to be on the best of terms with a mollusc.

This does not mean that I have any love for war. . . . But though I would fain hope that we may here do something to create and to maintain an Imperialism of peace, I cannot forget that we live in a world with which we are closely bound up, in which theories of economic self-sufficiency sometimes degenerate into predatory greed. How, in such a world, can we get the most fire insurance at the smallest cost? Surely only by closer union with the great congeries of states with which we are historically connected; not by independence, but by interdependence. . . .

We are part of this work-a-day world, and we cannot get out of it. We must take our part in the great congeries of states with which we are inter-related, and we can do so best by working along the line of historic connection. We are not going to be dependent; we are not going to be independent; we must be something more than a hermit crab, cowering in a shell we have done nothing to create; but we will find the development we need not in Nationalism, but in Imperialism, not in independence, but in interdependence. The independence of which Mr. Ewart and Mr. Bourassa dream would be only a form of servitude; only by interdependence can you achieve such independence as is possible in this world of ours.

Part II

The Critique of
Imperialism

The Boer War was the traumatic event that galvanized the anti-imperialists into action. While it is true that the movement for imperial unity did not march unopposed during the later eighties and early nineties, that it had in fact encountered substantial opposition and indifference, it was only after 1900 that anti-imperialism as an organized counterattack emerged and grew in strength.

Anti-imperialism found its most enduring basis of support in French Canada and it came to be symbolized by one man—Henri Bourassa. Bourassa, the grandson of Joseph-Louis Papineau, was thirty-one and a rising star in the Liberal party when he parted company with Laurier over the sending of Canadian contingents to South Africa, and from 1899 onwards his critique of imperialism as reactionary, anti-Canadian and racialist never ceased. There were others in the *Ligue Nationaliste,* like Olivar Asselin or Armand Lavergne, whose contributions to the definition of the aims of French Canadian nationalism were often more constructive than Bourassa's, but it was "O'Bourassa" that was sung to the tune of O'Canada by the students and it was "Bourassa the Dirty" who was so vehemently denounced in certain circles in English Canada.

Bourassa's critique of imperialism rested upon his view of Canadian history, the postulates of Manchester liberalism, and an interpretation of the imperial impulse which had been popularized by its English opponents. Bourassa believed that Canada's participation in the Boer War had established a precedent for the future and it meant that Joseph Chamberlain could call upon her aid in any and all subsequent imperial conflicts. This "constitutional revolution" was inimical to Canadian freedom of action and a denial of her history. For one hundred and fifty years Canada had loosened the ties that had bound her to Britain, and, mainly through the struggles of Mackenzie and Papineau,

Baldwin and La Fontaine, her people secured the right of governing themselves. Left alone, this development could have only one logical outcome—independence. The action of 1899 was, for Bourassa, an attempt to stop and reverse the tide of history. In 1902 Bourassa said that he was content to let the relationship between Britain and Canada remain exactly as it stood. The first point in the agenda of the *Ligue Nationaliste* read: "For Canada, in its relations with Great Britain, the largest measure of autonomy campatible with the maintenance of the colonial bond." Though he personally looked forward to independence in the distant future, Bourassa thought it unrealistic to expect an independent nationality when her two peoples were so divided, divided moreover, by their very different reactions to imperialism itself.

Beneath this interpretation of imperialism as antithetical to self-government and eventual independence lay the conviction that in essence the movement was economic in motivation and that it was intended to serve Britain's, not Canada's, interests. Like John Hobson, the English author of *Imperialism A Study (1902)*, one of the most influential analyses of imperialism, Bourassa traced the drive for imperial unity back to financial and commercial circumstances, particularly to the fall in trade returns and the loss of Britain's industrial supremacy to the United States and Germany. The real meaning of Chamberlain's campaign, disguised as it might temporarily be in the rhetoric of jingoism and invocations to the white man's burden, was to arrest Britain's relative decline by securing certain markets, raw materials and food supplies in the colonies. In return for a trifling preference on Canadian wheat the British imperialists demanded that Canada give military and naval support to the Empire. To Bourassa this appeared to be a gross and vulgar bargain: he defined imperialism as "MILITARY CONTRIBUTIONS FROM THE COLONIES TO GREAT BRITAIN, in men and treasure, but mainly in men."

Bourassa had a very rational and unemotional, some said calculating, view of the British connection, and he had no illusions regarding the motives underlying the shifts and changes in British policy in the past. While not unmindful of advantages that Canada had gained through the imperial association, he also remembered and underscored the repeated attempts to anglicize his people and the lamentable record of British diplomacy in sacrificing Canadian interests.

In the first selection reprinted here Bourassa attempted to explain why French Canadians could not possibly look upon the British connection and hence imperialism in the same way as their English Canadian fellow citizens; in the second selection he expressed his fear that in spite of these objections, military and economic imperialism might fuse and triumph together. The French Canadian nationalists made many attempts to explain their views to English Canadians. One of the most successful attempts at doing so was made by Olivar Asselin, from 1904 to 1908 the editor of *Le Nationaliste*, the press organ of the nationalist movement until the founding of *Le Devoir* in 1910. The section of his explanation that appears here represents a direct refutation, almost point by point, of George Foster's plea for naval preparedness.

The opposition to imperialism did not come from French Canada alone, though some imperialists talked as though it did. Two of the major English Canadian critics of the movement were Adam Shortt and John S. Ewart. Shortt was one of Canada's pioneer economic historians, and from 1891 to 1908, when he joined the Civil Service Commission, he taught political economy at Queen's. In 1904, the year after Chamberlain resigned

from the cabinet to crusade for imperial preference, Shortt published a searching dissection of that proposal. Canadian manufacturers had always been opposed to any scheme for imperial unity which threatened to throw open the Canadian market to British manufactured goods, but Shortt stated the case against preferential trade in terms far broader than self-interest alone. In a direct reply to those who shared Denison's convictions, Shortt drew out the implications of such a policy. Canada, he said, would have to give up industrialism and remain content in a kind of stultified, economic servitude.

John Ewart's line of reasoning was constitutional rather than economic. He was a lawyer who had argued the case of the Catholic minority of Manitoba for separate, state-supported schools, and, like Bourassa, he believed that racial harmony and understanding was the primary condition for national unity. In a closely argued series of essays, which were published as *The Kingdom Papers* in 1912 and 1914, Ewart cut through the obscurities and inflated rhetoric that surrounded the question of Canada's actual status. He contended that in every particular, including control over legislation and economic and foreign policy, Canada was independent, and that no Canadian imperialist questioned that fact. The only link between Canada and Britain was a common king; the only way to end the confusion about Canadian status was a straightforward declaration that Canada was an independent kingdom which had the same monarch as Great Britain. Just as Ewart shared Bourassa's opinion that the animating drive behind imperialism was economic profit, so too Bourassa hailed Ewart's exposition of Canada's real status as one of the finest contributions to Canadian nationalism.

Henri Bourassa, "The French-Canadian in the British Empire," *The Monthly Review,* Vol. IX (Oct. 1902), pp. 53-68.

Why French Canadians

Oppose Imperialism

The present feeling of the French-Canadian is one of contentment. He is satisfied with his lot. He is anxious to preserve his liberty and his peace. . . . Upon any proposed modification of the constitutional system of Canada he is disposed to look with distrust, or at least with anxiety. He cannot forget that all changes in the past were directed against him, except those that were enacted under such peculiar circumstances as made it imperative for the British Government to conciliate him. He asks for no change— for a long time to come, at least. And should any change be contemplated, he is prepared to view it, to appreciate its prospective advantages and inconveniences, neither from a British point of view nor from his own racial standpoint, but to approach the problem as it may affect the exclusive interests of Canada. He has loyally accepted the present constitution; he has done his ample share of duty by the country; and he feels that he is entitled to be consulted before any change is effected.

How thoroughly and exclusively Canadian the French-Canadian is should never be forgotten by those who contemplate any change in the constitutional or national status of Canada. This is so patent a fact, so logical a consequence of historical developments, that nothing short of absolute ignorance or wilful blindness can justify the language of those who talk of drawing him either by persuasion or by force to a closer allegiance to the Empire. As a matter of fact, he constitutes the only exclusively Canadian racial group in the Dominion. A constant immigration from the British Isles has kept the English-speaking Canadians in close contact with their motherland; so that even now they still speak of the "Old Country" as their "home," thus keeping in their hearts a double allegiance. On the soil of Canada, his only home and country, all the national aspirations of the French-Canadian are concentrated. "Canadian" is the only national designation he ever claims; and when he calls himself "French-Canadian," he simply wants to differentiate his racial origin from that of his English, Scotch, or Irish fellow citizen, who, in his mind, are but partially *Canadianised.*

When he is told that Canada is a British country, and that he must abide by the will of the British majority, he replies that Canada has remained British through his own loyalty; that when his race constituted the overwhelming majority of the Canadian people, Canada was twice saved to the British Crown, thanks to him and to him only; that he has remained faithful to Great Britain because he was assured of certain rights and privileges; that his English-speaking fellow citizens have accepted the compact and should not now take advantage of their greater numerical strength to break the agreement; that when settling in Canada,

newcomers from the British kingdom should understand that they become citizens of Canada, of a Confederacy where he has vested rights, and should not undertake to make the country and its people more British than Canadian. . . .

Independence is to his mind the most natural outcome of the ultimate destinies of Canada. But so long as the present ties are not strengthened he is in no hurry to sever British connection. He realises that time cannot but work in favour of Canada by bringing to her population and wealth, and that the later she starts on her own course the safer the journey. . . . .

Now, apart from his instinctive reluctance to contemplate any political evolution, what are the feelings of the French-Canadian with regard to Imperial Federation or any form of British Imperialism?

First, as may be naturally expected, sentimental arguments in favour of British Imperialism cannot have any hold upon him. To his reason only must appeals on this ground be made. That the new Imperial policy will bring him, and Canada at large, advantages that will not be paid by any infringement on his long-struggled-for liberty, he must be clearly shown.

Towards Great Britain he knows that he has a duty of allegiance to perform. But he understands that duty to be what it has been so far, and nothing more. He has easily and generously forgotten the persecutions of the earlier and larger part of his national life under the British Crown. He is willing to acknowledge the good treatment which he has received later on, though he cannot forget that his own tenacity and the neighbourhood of the United States have had much to do with the improvement of his situation.

In short, his affection for Great Britain is one of reason, mixed with a certain amount of esteem and suspicion, the proportions of which vary according to time and circumstances, and also with his education, his temperament, and his social surroundings.

Towards the Empire he has no feelings whatever; and naturally so. The blood connection and the pride in Imperial power and glory having no claims upon him, what sentiment can he be expected to entertain for New Zealand or Australia, South Africa or India, for countries and populations entirely foreign to him, with which he has no relations, intellectual or political, and much less commercial intercourse than he has with the United States, France, Germany, or Belgium?

By the motherland he feels that he has done his full duty; by the Empire he does not feel that he has any duty to perform. He makes full allowance for the blood feelings of his English-speaking partner; but having himself, in the past, sacrificed much of his racial tendencies for the sake of Canadian unity, he thinks that the Anglo-Canadian should be prepared to study the problems of Imperialism from a purely Canadian standpoint. Moreover, this absence of racial feelings from his heart allows him to judge more impartially the question of the relations between Canada and the Empire.

He fully realises the benefits that Canada derives from her connection with a wealthy and mighty nation. He is satisfied with having the use of the British market. But this advantage he knows that Canada enjoys on the very same terms as any other country in the world, even the most inimical to Britain. From a mixed sense of justice and egotism he is less clamorous than the British Canadian in demanding any favour, commercial or

other, from the motherland, because he has a notion that any favour received would have to be compensated by at least an equal favour given.

His ambition does not sway him to huge financial operations. Rather given to liberal professions, to agricultural life, or to local mercantile and industrial pursuits, he is more easily satisfied than the English-speaking Canadian with a moderate return for his work and efforts. He has been kept out of the frantic display of financial energy, of the feverish concentration of capital, of the international competition of industry, which have drawn his English-speaking fellow citizen to huge combinations of wealth or trade; and therefore, he is not anxious to participate in the organisation of the Empire on the basis of a gigantic co-operative association for trade. He would rather see Canada keep the full control of her commercial policy and enter into the best possible trade arrangements with any nation, British or foreign.

He is told that Canada has the free use of British diplomacy, and that such an advantage calls for sacrifices on her part when Britain is in distress. But considered in the light of past events, British diplomacy has, on the contrary, cost a good deal to Canada. So far the foreign relations of Canada, through British mediation, have been almost exclusively confined to America. That the influence and prestige of Great Britain were of great benefit to Canada in her relations with the United States is hardly conspicuous in the various Anglo-American treaties and conventions in which Canadian interests are concerned.

Not only did the American Republic secure the settlement of nearly all her claims according to her pretentions, but Canadian rights have been sacrificed by British plenipotentiaries in compensation for misdeeds or blunders of the British Government.

In fact, the Reciprocity Treaty of 1854 stands as the only convention entered into by Great Britain and the United States in which Canada stood at an advantage. But when the Secession War came, Great Britain gave to the slave-owning States a half-hearted moral support, too weak to turn the tide of fortune on their side, but strong enough to raise the ire of the victorious Government. Canada paid the price of revenge. Not only was the treaty of 1854 denounced, never to be renewed, but in the Washington Treaty of 1871 Canadian fisheries were made accessible to the Americans at a time when they were most profitable, in order to reconcile the United States and pay for the protection offered by Great Britain to privateers of the Southern States. True, Canada was awarded a money compensation; but the United States was none the less given a valuable privilege within the limits of Canadian territory, and one upon which the Canadian Government had always relied to procure trade reciprocity with the Americans. This unfair transaction was strenuously opposed by Sir John A. Macdonald, Prime Minister of Canada, who acted on that occasion as one of the British plenipotentiaries. He went to the length of threatening either to resign or to withold the sanction of the Canadian Parliament from the treaty. At last he gave way under the pressure of his colleagues, Lord de Grey, Sir Stafford Northcote, and Sir Edward Thornton, who convinced him that Canadian rights had to be sacrificed for the sake of Imperial interests.

Now with regard to disputes over boundaries. In the Treaty of 1842, where-

by the northern frontiers of the State of Maine were delimitated, a large portion of Canadian territory was abandoned to the Americans by Lord Ashburton, who jocosely observed that he did not care for a few degrees of latitude more or less. Later on, the Oregon boundaries were also fixed in a way which Canada claimed was unjust to her; although it must be admitted that this time the Americans endeavoured to get more territory than they actually secured. Not later than last year the Clayton-Bulwer convention was denounced without any settlement of the Alaskan boundary being reached. Canada had no right under that treaty; but she always claimed that the anxiety of the United States for its removal offered a most propitious occasion for a fair application in her favour of the famous Monroe doctrine, so dear to the heart of the Americans. Great Britain waiving her rights in a treaty dealing with questions of a purely American nature—in the geographical sense—Canada rightly expected that this abandonment should be compensated by the settlement of another exclusively American problem. This view was strongly urged by the Canadian authorities upon the Home Government; it has even been stated that this was one of the primary conditions of the unfruitful negotiations carried on at Quebec and Washington in 1898-1899, under the presidency of Lord Herschel, but evidently all in vain.

It may be argued that all those concessions, made by Great Britain at the expense of Canada, were imposed by circumstances. It may be said also that by those same concessions Canada at large was affected, and that the French-Canadians had no greater cause of complaint than their English-speaking fellow citizens. But that exclusive Canadian sentiment which I have described makes the French-Canadian feel more deeply any encroachment upon the integrity of Canada. Unlike the Anglo-Canadian, he does not find in the glory of Empire a compensation and a solace for the losses suffered by Canada. That he entertains any rancour against Britain on that account would, however, be a false conclusion. For the international intricacies in which Great Britain has been and is still entangled he makes full allowance. With his strong sense of self-government, he does not expect the motherland to endanger her own position on behalf of Canada. But if Great Britain is either unable or unwilling to take risks for the sake of Canadian interests, he does not see why Canada should assume new obligations towards Great Britain and run risks on her behalf.

As far as war and defence are concerned, he is still less disposed to consent to any Imperial combination. First there is that aversion to militarism that I have mentioned. Then he has a notion that all the sacrifices he may make on this ground will be so much that Canada will give without any probable return.

When he turns towards the past, what does he find? He finds that for the hundred and forty years that he has been a British subject, no more than his English-speaking fellow citizen has he ever been the cause, near or distant, of any trouble to Great Britain. Never did Canada involve the Empire in any war or threat of war. But the policy, right or wrong, of the British Government did cause his country to be the battlefield of two Anglo-American struggles. Upon those two occasions Canada was saved to the British Crown, thanks to the loyalty of his own race. During the Secession

war, the peace of Canada came very near being disturbed once more, and her territory was threatened with invasion because of the attitude of Great Britain. And if he has been spared this and other bloody contests, it was only by the granting to the United States of such concessions as are referred to above.

So much for the past. When he considers the present and the future, the French-Canadian does not see any reason why he should enter into a scheme of Imperial defence.

The argument that if Canada stands by the Empire, the Empire will stand by Canada, cannot have much weight with him; and his objections on that ground are founded both on past events and on prospective developments. In the South African War he has witnessed an application of the new doctrine. Of the expenditure of that war he has been called upon to pay his share—a small one if compared with that of the British Kingdom, but a large one when it is remembered that he had no interest whatever in the contest, and no control over the policy which preceded the conflict, or over its settlement. Should the principle of military Imperialism predominate, he foresees that he may find himself involved in wars occasioned by friction between Australia and Japan, between New Zealand and Germany, between Great Britain and France in Europe, or between Great Britain and Russia in Asia. He does not see any eventuality in which the Empire may be called upon to help Canada.

He is ready now, as he was in the past, to support a sufficient military force to maintain internal peace and to resist aggression on the territory of Canada. But these eventualities are most unlikely to occur in the near future. The enormous area as well as the vast resources of the country offer such opportunities to the care and activity of its population, that social struggles are almost impossible in Canada for many years to come. Foreign invasion, from the United States excepted, is most improbable. The Canadian territory is easy to defend against attacks on her sea borders, which would offer great difficulties and little benefit to any enemy of the Empire. Moreover, from a purely Canadian standpoint such occurrences are most unlikely to happen. Left to herself Canada has no possible cause of conflict with any other nation but the United States. On the other hand, by entering into a compact for Imperial defence, she may be involved in war with several of the strongest Powers. Therefore, as far as concerns any country outside America, the French-Canadian feels that the scheme of Imperial defence brings upon him new causes of conflict not to be compensated by any probable defensive requirement.

It is worthwhile mentioning here one possible conflict in which, if Imperialism carries the day, the racial problem of Canada might cause serious trouble. Although happily checked by a large interchange of material interests, the possibility of a war between France and Great Britain is not altogether removed. Were such a conflict confined to these two Powers, the French-Canadian could be counted upon to stand loyally neutral. Should even the French navy, by the most improbable of war fortunes, attack the coast of Canada, the French-Canadian could be relied upon for the defence of his country. But should the principle of Imperial solidarity obtain, were Canada called upon to contribute to an Anglo-French war in which she had no direct interest, the French-Canadian would no doubt resent most bitterly any such contribution in men or money as could be voted by the Federal Parliament.

This would no longer be the defence of his home—which he is prepared to undertake even against France—it would mean his contributing to the slaughter of his own kith and kin in a quarrel which was foreign to him. It would hurt the French-Canadian in that most peculiar and sentimental love for the French national soul which I have already mentioned.

There remains to be dealt with the eventuality of a war with the United States. Rightly or wrongly, the French-Canadian is inclined to think that, in order to avert such a calamity, Great Britain would even go to the length of abandoning all British rights in America. And should British sentiment and British policy undergo such a change as would warrant Canada in counting upon the armed help of the Empire against the United States, the French-Canadian entertains some doubt as to the possibility of keeping up the struggle and carrying it to a successful issue.

Should the most sanguine expectations be realised; should the American Navy be annihilated even as a defence force; and were the British Navy to succeed in blockading and bombarding the American ports—the only effective blow which might be struck at the enemy—nothing could prevent the American army from occupying the central portion of Canada, and probably invading most of her territory. Canada would therefore, at all events, be the sufferer in the fight. Moreover, her ways of transportation from the Western graingrowing country would be interrupted; and whilst the Americans would get from their untouched territory unbounded resources of food supply, the British people would be at once deprived of American and Canadian breadstuffs. This alone, in spite of any military success in other ways, would force Great Britain to accept the terms of the American Republic.

Another point to be considered with reference to an Anglo-American War is the fact that there are now as many French-Canadians living under the star-spangled banner as under the Union Jack. Many of those migrated Canadians have become as loyal and devoted citizens of the American Republic as their brothers have remained loyal and devoted citizens of Canada. Although prepared to do his full duty in the defence of his land, the prospect of his becoming the murderer of his own brother is sufficient to prevent the French-Canadian from exposing Canada and the Empire to any war with the United States.

From all those considerations the French-Canadian concludes that Canada has never been, and never will be, the cause of any display of Imperial strength, with the single exception of a possible encounter with a nation that he is not desirous of attacking, and against which, in his mind, the Empire would be either unwilling or incapable of defending him. He does not therefore feel bound to assume military obligations towards any other part of the Empire.

The stronger Canada grows in population and wealth, the slighter will be the dangers that may threaten her security, and the greater her contribution to the welfare and glory of the Empire. The French-Canadian thinks therefore that the best way in which he can play his part in the building up of the Empire is not by diverting the healthiest and strongest portion of its population from the pursuits of a peaceful and industrious life and sending them to fight in all parts of the world. He does not believe in fostering in Canada the spirit of militarism. He is only anxious to make his country attractive and pros-

perous by keeping aloof from all military adventures.

Indifferent as he is to commercial Imperialism, hostile as he is to military Imperialism, the French-Canadian cannot be expected to wish for any organic change in the constitution of Canada and to look favourably upon any scheme of Imperial Federation.

For years he fought to obtain full control of his laws, of his social system, of his public exchequer. With the principles of self-government, of self-taxation, of direct control over the legislative body, no other citizen of the British Empire is more thoroughly imbued than he is. His local organisation, in Church, educational or municipal matters, is still more decentralised and democratic than that of the English provinces of Canada. He likes to exercise his elective franchise and to keep as close as possible to the man, the law and the regulation that he votes for. He cannot view with favour a scheme by which any power that has heretofore been exercised by his own representative bodies may pass under the control of some Council sitting in London.

There remains to be considered the question of annexation to the United States.

As I have stated, left to himself, the French-Canadian is not eager for a change. He requires nothing but quietness and stability in order to grow and develop. He is satisfied with and proud of his Canadian citizenship. But should a change be forced upon him by those who aspire to a greater nationality, he would rather incline towards Pan-Americanism.

For a long time annexation to the United States was most abhorrent to the French-Canadian. In fact, when an agitation in that direction was started by several leading English-speaking Cana-

dians, his resistance proved to be the best safeguard of the British connection. But should his past fidelity be now disregarded, and Canadian autonomy encroached upon in any way, should he be hurried into any Imperial scheme and forced to assume fresh obligations, he would prefer throwing in his lot with his powerful neighbour to the South. His present constitution he prizes far above the American system of Government; but if called upon to sacrifice anything of his Federal autonomy for the working of the Imperial machinery, he would rather do it in favour of the United States system, under which, at all events, he would preserve the self-government of his province. Should Imperial re-organisation be based on trade and financial grounds, he would see a greater future in joining the most powerful industrial nation of the world than in going into partnership with the British communities; and this sentiment is gaining greater force from the present influx of American capital into Canada. The fact that the union of Canada and the United States would bring again under the same flag the two groups, now separated, of his nationality has no doubt greatly contributed towards smoothing his aversion to annexation.

I have so far analysed the sentiments of the higher classes among the French-Canadian people, of those who control their feelings by historical knowledge or by a study of outside circumstances, political, military or financial. If I refer to the masses, mostly composed of farmers, I may say that they entertain similar feelings, but instinctively rather than from reflection. The French-Canadians of the polular class look upon Canada as their own country. They are ready to do their duty by Canada; but considering they owe nothing to Great Britain or any other

country, they ask nothing from them. Imbued with a strong sense of liberty, they have no objection to their English-speaking fellow countrymen going to war anywhere they please; but they cannot conceive that Canada as a whole may be forced out of its present situation. They let people talk of any wise and wild proposal of Imperialism; but if any change were attempted to be imposed on them, they would resist the pressure, quietly but constantly.

To sum up, the French-Canadian is decidedly and exclusively Canadian by nationality and American by his ethnical temperament. People with world-wide aspirations may charge him with provincialism. But after all, this sentiment of exclusive attachment to one's land and one's nationality is to be found as one of the essential characteristics of all strong and growing peoples. On the other hand, the lust of abnormal expansion and Imperial pride have ever been the marked features of all nations on the verge of decadence.

Henri Bourassa, *Great Britain and Canada Topics of the Day A Lecture Delivered at the "Théatre National Français," Montreal, On the 20th of October 1901,* (Montreal, C. O. Beauchemin et Fils, 1902), pp. 4, 11-12, 15-17, 19, 25-26, 28-31. Reprinted by permission of Beauchemin Ltée.

The Economic Taproot of

British Imperialism

British Imperialism—as opposed to British democracy, to British traditions, to British grandeur—is a lust for land-grabbing and military dominion. Born of the overgrowth of British power, bred by that stupid and blatant sense of pride known as *Jingoism,* it delights in high-sounding formulas:—*"Britannia, rule the waves!"* . . . *"Britons never shall be slaves!"* . . . *"Trade follows the Flag"* . . . *"What we have, we hold!"* . . . ; to this last axiom, the Prime-Minister of Ontario has added:—*"and what we don't have, we take"* —which is now supplemented by public good sense by: *"when we can."*

Having undertaken more responsibilities than she is able to stand, surrounded as she is by hostile or indifferent nations, the new Britain of Mr. Chamberlain is in sore need of soldiers and sailors to prop the fabric raised by her frantic ambition. Being actually denuded of troops at home, she turns in distress to her colonies. Realising as they do that without practising evasion they cannot possibly achieve their purpose, British rulers of to-day resort to deceit and bribery with colonial statesmen; they lull the credulity and inflame the jingo feelings of the people of the colonies. Under miscellaneous names and variegated uniforms— Royal Rifles, Mounted Infantry, Strathcona Horse, Yeomanry—they extort from us whatever they may get in the shape of human material for their army; even if they have to dangle before our eyes a few paltry advantages to be thrown as a sop to us whenever we get tired of this deadly game.

In short, MILITARY CONTRIBŪTIONS FROM THE COLONIES TO GREAT BRITAIN, in men and treasure, but mainly in men, constitute British Imperialism. . . .

All Empires, modern or ancient, were born of some political or military idea. They were the outcome of conquests or treaties contrived, undertaken, conducted or achieved by conquerors, statesmen, rulers and diplomatists. And history bears witness to the fact that, as a rule, those political structures collapsed with their authors or their successors, whether single or collective.

The British Empire, on the contrary, was built up and developed like the British constitution, outside of any general theory or preconcerted plan of action, without government help and often contrary to the wishes of the Crown and the sense of the people.

Go back to the history of the thirteen American colonies, to that of India, of Australia, or New Zealand, and you will find that those countries were built up by English settlers and shop-keepers, by political or sectarian refugees and discharged convicts. Of these some were in quest of peace and liberty, others, of wealth; some had turned in anger from the parent's roof, cursing the men and institutions of

their country; others, indifferent to all the rest, cared only for pelf. To none of these pioneers did it ever occur that he was endowing his country with an empire. . . .

Let us go back to the American colonies. Here again crops up the same reluctance to territorial acquisition. However, the prosperity of the colonies and their commercial intercourse with the traders of the Mother country, finally compelled the attention of the home government, and, as was the case with India, brought about official recognition. This resulted in the creation of the several colonial constitutions whereby His Britannic Majesty, while accepting the allegiance of his subjects over-seas, left them to bear the burden of self-government, taxation and defence.

From a strange obliteration of historical sense, which often leads to a confusion of the ideas of cause and effect, we have come to the conclusion that these constitutions were the work of the far-seeing genius of England. As a matter of fact, a provision which imposed upon the colonies almost all the burdens and responsibilities of their own government, was, in the mind of her statesmen, the onerous consideration for which the colonists were granted the signal privilege of being admitted to the rank of His Majesty's subjects.

Upon that principle of decentralisation,—a principle quite novel, and essentially antagonistic to the paternalism of the colonial empires of Spain, Portugal and France,—was built up the British Empire, and the day came when that little island to the north of Europe ruled the widest area of scattered lands that ever acknowledged one single authority. It is then no paradox to state that of the anti-imperialistic sense of the English people was born the British Empire, and that in the strength of that instinct lies the secret of its maintenance.

However, the first germs of Imperialism were soon to develop, and, possibly, this was bound to happen. It is with nations who colonise before making conquests as with those who make conquests before colonising: the moment comes when they are confronted by an identical situation, with a colonial empire for the defence of which they have to provide. . . .

The British government attempted to force the American colonies to share in the costs of their own defence and of the Seven-Years' war. From this first move towards political imperialism resulted the momentous event which gave birth to one of the greatest of modern world-powers. Such a sudden reaction benefited both Great Britain and Canada. Realising the wish of Lord Chatham, the American Revolution checked the progress of imperialism in Great Britain. It ushered in the era of our political emancipation and constitutional liberty. . . .

After half a century of struggles you are familiar with, the acute stage of which was reached in 1837, we finally secured responsible government and provincial autonomy. . . .

The campaign of Cobden, with the triumph of free-trade, was another timely circumstance which strengthened our new-born liberties. An immense impetus was given to British trade, and the former artisan of Manchester became the prophet of Great Britain. To Cobden, Imperialism, both military and political, was abhorrent; colonial expansion he distrusted. In the remote possessions of England he foresaw a source of dangers abroad and within; in the infinitude of colonial and foreign questions engrossing the attention of Parliament, an impediment to social reform; in the necessity of an army and a

war fleet, a bold defiance of foreign powers, and an insuperable obstacle to the fulfilment of his two most cherished dreams, free-trade and universal peace.

The endorsation of his system by the English people he failed to secure, but he succeeded in spreading enough of his doctrine to enlist their support in favour of a policy of complete colonial decentralisation as an initial step towards secession. His comparison—after Turgot—of the ripe fruit dropping from the tree, became the familiar image by which rulers and subjects realised the Empire. The colonies were given to understand that they were to be self-reliant and self-supporting, and that whensoever they thought fit to sever their connection with the motherland, no obstacle would be put in the way.

While we were enjoying an absolute security, and getting used to this large measure of independence, the remembrance of the heavy price paid for our liberty began to vanish. Out of colonial expansion were soon to grow new germs of that political and military Imperialism, which had been checked by the American Revolution, and retarded by the influence of Cobden. . . .

. . . In the economical and military situation of Great Britain, Mr. Chamberlain finds a field of action, interested co-operators, and arguments far more forcible than the homilies of those who worship at the shrine of an Empire upon which the sun is never allowed to set.

But unquestionably it is with free trade as with any other political system which does not extend beyond the sphere of material interests: whether it be true or beneficial altogether depends upon its endorsation by the majority. In Cobden's own mind, not until, following in the footsteps of England, all the other nations should have thrown their gates wide open to the world was his work to achieve perfection. Now, in this regard, the expectations of the great economist have been falsified.

The English producer has seen the civilised nations gradually closing their doors against him. His best customers, Germany and the United States, have boldly gone into extensive manufacturing. For some years the trade of Great Britain was not seriously hampered. Her vessels still went on carrying over the seas articles of consumption for the whole world. . . . But there came a time when, from the protective policy of the other industrial nations, flowed an unlooked-for result. After having realised enormous profits on their own markets, closed as they are to foreign competition, German and American manufacturers took to exporting their over-production to foreign markets, selling their goods with a bare margin of profit and even beneath the cost of production. . . .

Hence the British manufacturer stands confronted by the following conditions: his goods are shut out from the markets of the civilised world by protection, and from the open markets by foreign competition, whereas the needs of home consumption are amply supplied. He looks about, in quest of a remedy. He begins to question whether he had not sooner build up for himself a more modest abode than the world-palace in which he has so far dwelt as a supreme ruler. In order to secure a few markets which he might properly call his own, he would gladly consent to a few sacrifices of principle and even of treasure, to be shared in common with his fellow-citizens. To achieve that result he needs turn to countries where he could exercise some political authority. Only in the English colonies is such a situation to be found.

But *"give and take"* is the cardinal principle of good business relations, and of this the British manufacturer is well aware. He is the last man to believe that sentimental outbursts may be producive of permanent results. He foresees that when once they have outlived the period of fierce love, the Colonies will demand in return for their self-sacrifices more substantial rewards than medals and titles for their great men. Then it is that the problem bristles with difficulties.

Impoverished as he is, and over-burdened by direct taxation, the British rate-payer does not mean to tax his own food, that English plutocrats may acquire the estates of a ruined aristocracy, nor even to bestow favours upon his colonial kinsfolk, whose welfare is of far less moment to him than the problem of his every day meal. For it is the necessities of life that the Colonies have to sell him, and on which he may offer them a profit. On silk goods and wines from France, on toys and fancy articles from Germany, on art products from Italy, he would readily have duties levied; but neither would the English manufacturer nor the farmer from the Colonies benefit thereby. From every colony would come a demand to the British ratepayer to impose a duty: from Canada, on his lumber, breadstuffs, butter and eggs; from Australia and South Africa, on his wool and woollen goods, and his meat; from the West Indies, on his sugar, already taxed for the purpose of replenishing an empty public exchequer, a result of Messrs Rhodes' and Chamberlain's enterprises; to say nothing of the fact that he has long been paying double price for his tea and his ale, in order to maintain his army, navy and monarchy.

And thus it happens that for the purpose of extending a slight favour to the producers of each colony individually, the English consumer would be compelled to burden with taxes almost every staple article of consumption. . . .

From the question of taxation I am led to the study of British Imperialism as viewed from the standpoint of England's military position. . . .

Let England show herself in the least aggressive or exacting, and forthwith causes of conflict will crop up in every direction. In Egypt, in Afghanistan, in the Southern Seas, from the insolence of a clerk, from the blunder of a Consular agent, from the exigencies of any one of her Colonies, she may be forced into a war with France, Russia or Germany. Owing to the eclipse of her ascendency in China, she is already being made to pay by anticipation, and a hundred fold for all that the gold mines on the Rand and the diamonds of Kimberley could ever yield. England has learnt lessons from her South African misadventure, which she will remember; and, from a strictly military point of view, one of these object-lessons is that, brave as they are, British officers are inefficient, and that such recruits as she may now enlist do not deserve the name of soldiers, being, on the confession of Lord Kitchener himself, but a mere horde of cumbersome parasites.

Great Britain has always placed more reliance on her navy than on her army for the general defence of the Empire. . . . But is the British navy still able to cope with the combined fleets of any two other nations? For such is the principle laid down by the British authorities as the primary guarantee of the safety of the Empire; and such is the question, which being asked by many a well-informed Englishman, they all hesitate answering in the affirmative. That this same problem is being solved abroad in a much more pessimistic spirit as to Great Britain goes

without saying. I am not at all qualified to revise these calculations; but what may be asserted without rashness and without technical knowledge, is this, that it has grown out of fashion for the world at large to stand in awe of British power. Hence risks of Great Britain being involved in war have largely increased. . . .

. . . Great Britain is in sore need of recruits to fill the ranks of her army. Did she persist in discarding the ideas championed by Cobden, Bright and all those whom Mr. Chamberlain, in one of his frolicsome moods, nicknamed "little Englanders",—did she refuse to reverse her policy of militarism,—where is she going to find the necessary material to meet her deficiencies? Two resources only she has at her disposal; conscription, or an appeal to the Colonies, a resort to either of which would prove equally dangerous. . . .

Imperialists entertain the ultimate hope—and of all their theories this is perhaps the most plausible and the most dangerous to us—that at the critical moment the problem is to be solved by an amalgamation of military and economical imperialism. The British rate-payers would be induced to consent to increased taxation in favour of colonial products, by being led into the belief that the only alternative to the bugbear of conscription lies in this assistance of colonial legions. The Colonies, on the other hand, would be invited to fill the ranks of the army and navy by being offered trade advantages. To sum up the theory, the colonies are to purchase, by paying the tax of blood, the advantage of a preferential treatment in the [B]ritish market for their farm produce. Whether the contract be carried out or not, we may even now consider as a foregone conclusion that the balance of profit will not be in our favour.

Adam Shortt, *Imperial Preferential Trade from a Canadian Point of View* (Toronto, Morang & Co. Ltd., 1904), pp. 53-55, 57-59.

A Blighted, Bucolic Future for Canada as the Granary of the Empire

. . . That a manufacturing future is plainly not suited to our condition, is what Mr. Chamberlain insinuates in the most flattering terms. On grounds of sentiment, of imperial unity, and finally, of self-interest, we should be willing to leave the manufacturing to the Mother Country. But, in the first place, sentiment or loyalty affords a very precarious basis on which to do business, or, as in this case, to refrain from doing business. In fact, no more effective method of corrupting, and ultimately discrediting all imperial sentiment could be devised, than to begin trafficking on it. What the imperial preferential advocates, on the two sides of the Atlantic, are trying to do is to divide an expected mutual benefit in such a fashion, that each party shall receive about three-fourths of it, on the ground that the other must concede something extra for the sake of sentiment. A sample of the way in which each party manages to get the best of the bargain may be taken. In Canada we are encouraged to interpret the preference of six cents a bushel on wheat as meaning, that for every bushel of wheat we sell to Britain we shall get six cents more than formerly, or than we should have got without the preference. It is entirely on the strength of this that we are told our vacant lands will be settled. The people of Britain, however, are assured most earnestly that, notwithstanding the imposition of the proposed duty, the price of wheat will not be raised, since it can be shown very clearly that the foreigner pays the duty. In other words, while the price of wheat in Britain will remain practically what it was before the duty was imposed the foreigner will take less for his supply. But the British workman is further told, that the Canadian, in gratitude for not being taxed on his grain, and more particularly on account of his imperial enthusiasm, intends to open up his markets to British goods, devoting himself chiefly to growing wheat, and will thereby greatly increase work for the British artisan and augment his wage fund. Thus the foreigner will pay his taxes, and the colonial furnish him with wages, and his master with profits. As seen from the Canadian point of view, however, the only return which we are to make for the extra six cents a bushel on our wheat is, not to sacrifice our home market to Britain, but to so re-adjust our tariff that we shall divide between Britain and ourselves that portion of our trade which now goes to the foreigner, and the chief foreigner is, of course, the United States. But when we look at the details of our imports from the United States, and see how the millions are chiefly made up of payments for coal, raw cotton, corn, wheat, raw tobacco, cattle, and other live stock, petroleum, twine, carriages, machinery, settlers' effects, fish, farm implements, India rubber, coin and bullion, etc., etc., the irony of the situation is very fine,

and the imperial sentiment which infuses it all, is most suggestive of future unity and affection.

As attention is chiefly drawn in Canada to the expected benefits from the preference on wheat, we may look into that a little more closely. A duty of two shillings a quarter, or six cents a bushel, on foreign wheat imported into the British market, is expected to cause such a stream of immigration to set in to Canada, that it will fill up our North-West lands, make Canada the granary of the Empire, and in a few years render Britain independent of the rest of the world for her food supply. Now, in the first place, this implies that without some such premium on immigration, Canadian territory will attract few settlers, or, competing on even terms with the rest of the world, it must remain uninhabited. Now, though this idea has been published abroad, and emphasized in all sorts of ways in the interest of Imperialism, yet none more false or injurious to the reputation of the country could have been circulated. Any one who knows the facts knows that our lands have been taken up with unusual avidity. Settlement is taking place at a remarkable rate, and the lands are rapidly rising in value. Yet all this has been going on for some years without any preference at all, and is certain to continue in as great a measure as is at all safe or wise, until a series of poor harvests may be encountered, such as may come to any country, and which may check the rate of settlement for a time. . . .

Again, the ideal of becoming the granary of the Empire is constantly held up to Canada, both here and in Britain, as the guiding star of our ambition, the achievement of our destiny. Concerning this picture of our future, one may have the patience to say that any Canadian

who finds himself able to accept such an ideal must have a very curious conception of the real greatness of the British Empire, or what it means to have a self-respecting share in it. Doubtless, for all time, the world will cherish the glorious legacy of Athens; but what idea of Athenian greatness had those bucolic barbarians from the north who supplied the city with grain? Under suitable conditions rural life is quite consistent with the richest possibilities of civilization, as Britain herself proves. But the agricultural life, to be adequate, requires a varied industrial and commercial accompaniment, as a support for those elements of civilization which only towns and cities can supply, and in more or less intimate contact with which the best rural life must be developed. The agricultural life is followed by some of the highest and by some of the lowest types of humanity, and the actual sources of the British food supply well illustrate the social range of commercial agriculture. Outside of a few distributing centres, therefore, the people who make agriculture their national occupation must inevitably stagnate intellectually. Whatever spiritual capacities they may have will be lost to themselves and the world, for though they may vegetate they will neither blossom nor bear fruit.

Now, there is no virtue in belonging to the British Empire unless we have a share in its civilization, joining the Mother Country in its cosmopolitan intercourse with the leading nations of the world. But Canada, as the granary of the Empire, precludes all this for the immense majority of her people. Situated as our country is, it means that, in the course of time, most of the enterprising spirits born into the country will leave it, seeking the larger and fuller life elsewhere. Indeed, do we not know places in Canada to-day, where,

in virtue of two or three generations of culling out through the exodus, such a condition has been produced, that not even the trumpet of the angel of Gabriel could rouse the remaining population from its bucolic slumber?

But what is to be gained by making Canada the granary of the Empire? To this the usual answer is, that Britain may be insured a complete food supply from within her own Empire, and thus avoid all danger from starvation in time of war. But, if Britain is not at war in America, she will not be in any danger of starvation, under present conditions; and if she should be at war with the United States, it is obvious that her dependence upon Canada for her food supplies would be the most unfortunate situation conceivable. For, conceding to our warriors that Canada would have no difficulty in disposing of any possible American invasion of a general nature, yet it would not be difficult for a concentrated force from the United States, choosing its own point of attack over hundreds of miles, to seize and hold one or two positions on the line of communication between west and east, and thus permanently interrupt all transfers of grain from the interior to the sea. Obviously, the wisest policy for Britain, in view of possible wars, must be to maintain as large and varied a source of food supplies as possible. Equally wise is her present effort to enlarge her source of supply for cotton, or other important raw materials.

One need only suggest, also, what difficulties Britain would encounter, if she came to depend almost entirely upon Canada for bread, when, for any reason, there might be such a shortage of the wheat crop in the North-West as to leave Canada little more than enough for her own needs. Various other difficulties stand in the way of Canada being the granary of the Empire; but the supreme objection must ever be that Canada cannot accept for herself any such blighted destiny.

J. S. Ewart, "Canadian Independence," *The Kingdom Papers* (Ottawa, 1912) Vol. I, pp. 1-2, 8, 10-12, 16-20. The substance of this paper was delivered as a lecture in February, 1911, before the Canadian Clubs at London, Brantford, Hamilton and Kingston; the Women's Club at Kingston; and the Political Economy class at Queen's College.

The Kingdom of Canada

I am a Canadian nationalist. I may be doing you injustice, but I shall assume that a majority of you are not—that you would call yourselves imperialists. And the question that I wish to discuss is, whether there is any substantial difference between us? Or, perhaps, the better question would be: Is there any reason why an imperialist should not be a Canadian nationalist? I am firmly persuaded that there is no such reason. . . .

Now, probably, there is not a man in this room who would send Canada back to her colonial days; who would tolerate the exercise of controlling authority by our Governors-General; who would receive with submission, or accept without resentment, any appearance of dictation from the Colonial Office. Every one of you is in favor of Canadian self-government. Everyone is in favor of Canada being a nation. Well, that is what I call Canadian nationalism. . . .

. . . Practically we are in all respects independent: as to our fiscal relations, as to legislation, as to government, as to liti-

gation, as to treaties and as to war. Theoretically, we have no independent power. Practically, we are independent, and may do as we please. . . .

. . . The only real link, besides strong mutual sympathy—the only legal, or political, or constitutional, link that now connects Canada to the United Kingdom —is the Crown. . . .

. . . Not one of you would wish for the restoration of Downing Street rule. Not one would submit to our tariff being imposed upon us from London. Every one acknowledges allegiance to King George. May I not say that every man amongst you agrees to Canadian nationalism, when Canadian nationalism is understood as the equivalent of COMPLETE SELF-GOVERNMENT WITH KING GEORGE AS OUR SOVEREIGN?

But you have a question that you want to put to me: "Does Mr. Ewart advocate complete separation from the Empire?" In reply I say that I no more advocate separation from the United Kingdom, or other parts of the Empire, fiscally, legislatively, or governmentally, than geographically. Every one of them is an accomplished and irreversible fact. And the question that I return is: Does anybody advocate anything else? Does anyone desire that any fragment of our independence should be surrendered? Do not ask me, therefore, if I advocate separation. From the earliest days of our colonial history until very recently, we did struggle for self-government. No one need advocate it now. We have it; and we intend to keep it; and indeed, no one even suggests that we should part with it.

"But does Mr. Ewart advocate breaking up the Empire?" The answer is the same as I have just given. I advocate nothing of the kind. It would be absurd to do so, for as far as Canada is con-

cerned, the Empire—speaking politically and precisely—is already broken up; and no one proposes that it should be re-established, at all events in its original form. While Canada was a colony of the United Kingdom, Canada was a British possession. She was a part of the world governed by the British parliament, and she was, therefore, part of the British Empire. Now, practically, she is not. She is a separate and independent state. She is not governed by the British parliament. She has no political connection with the United Kingdom except that they have the same King. . . .

The nature of the present legal relation between the two countries is very simple. Each is a kingdom, and both have the same King. Neither has any authority over the other. . . .

The next questions very naturally, are these: If Canada really is practically independent, what more do we want? and why do we want it?

Gentlemen, I venture to say that what we want is what we have earned, namely, the title which properly describes us. We want our position acknowledged, not merely by individual British statesmen, but officially by the British parliament. If we have ceased to be a colony, we want to drop the word. If we are really a kingdom, we want that title as our designation. If we are equal in authority with the British parliament, we want that great achievement acknowledged. I, for one, see no reason why we should continue to be called a colony, or a "dominion beyond the seas," when in reality, we are nothing of the kind. I can understand a man ambitious of a designation superior to that to which he is entitled. I do not understand why anybody should be anxious to grovel along under a title inferior to that which he has properly and creditably won.

Are we a nation? If so, let us say it officially, as well as unofficially. I entirely agree with Professor Leacock, the Rhodes Imperialistic Missionary, when he says:

"The colonial status is a worn-out, bygone thing. The sense and feeling of it has become harmful to us. It limits the ideas, and circumscribes the patriotism of our people. It impairs the mental vigor, and narrows the outlook of those that are reared and educated in our midst."

For my part I dislike, most heartily, any badge of inferiority. In official documents we are styled "colonies," or "self-governing dominions," or "self-governing dependencies," or "our self-governing possessions" or "our over-sea dominions.". . .

I dislike that language. I resent it. I want to end it. I am not satisfied that Canada should occupy a place in the world inferior to that held by dozens of nations who cannot compare with her in wealth, strength, or intelligence. At international councils, Canada has no place, although all the little Republics of Central America and the comparatively insignificant kingdoms of Europe take rank there as though they were of some importance in the world. Montenegro, with less than half a million of inhabitants is a Kingdom; and so is Iceland. Canada is a colony.

And, gentlemen, I may say to you that the more reflective of the Imperialists not only agree in the reasonableness of dropping the word "colony" and of recognizing Canadian aspirations, but, as you may have gathered from some of the extracts which I have read, they actually advocate it as the only basis upon which any real union between Canada and the United Kingdom can be arranged. . . .

Passing to another point, I feel sure

that some of you wish to say to me that if we were independent, we could not maintain our independence; that Japan, or the United States would gobble us up. But observe that I have not proposed to change the present situation, but only to recognize it; and, therefore, that the only questions raised by the suggestion of being gobbled are; first, What is the present situation? and, secondly, How would the situation be affected by recognizing it?

The present situation may be summed up in a single sentence: We are in no danger, and if we were, we have no assurance of British assistance. Until the German scare is well over, the United Kingdom will not engage in war with the United States, or (for still stronger reasons) with Japan. The United Kingdom has not a single battleship on the Pacific, and for years to come will not send one there. Let us recognize the facts—the United Kingdom is, at present, much too anxious over her own position to undertake responsibilities on behalf of Canada. And Canada has no right to complain. She has declined to give the United Kingdom any assurance of help in case of war, and in return she has received none. We must keep the peace with Japan and the United States, or ourselves face the consequences. At all events my point, and my only point, is that we have no assurance of co-operation in case of trouble. . . .

. . . As long as our present anomalous relationship with the United Kingdom continues, we incur the danger of being attacked because of quarrels with which we have no connection. We have fought in various wars, and every one of them was of that description. There has

never been a war upon Canadian account. Independence would place our war-relationship upon known and reasonable footing. We should have specific and definite alliance, or we should not. The present situation is unfair to us in every way. We are expected to assist in every British war, and we have not the slightest assurance that any of our quarrels will be thought of sufficient importance to warrant war.

That is the present position. Now what would be the effect of making the theoretical conform to the practical? The chief benefit to be derived from a frank facing of the real facts of the situation (and I ask particular attention to this point) is that it would necessitate the removal of the uncertainties to which I have just referred. At present we have no agreement providing for cases of international difficulty. A declaration of our independence would sharply call our attention to that fact, and produce some line of definite action with reference to the most important feature of national life, namely, national safety. . . .

In other ways, too, a frank acknowledgement of the situation will be of the greatest possible benefit. Apart altogether from the extremely important advantage of enhanced self-respect, it will give us a unity, a cohesion, and a solidarity which we have not now. At present we are English, Scotch, Irish, French, American, etc. We ought to be Canadians. Eight hundred miles of rock and water separate our east from our west. We want a bond of union. . . .

. . . National sentiment is the only secure bulwark of national existence. We shall never have it as long as we remain a colony.

Olivar Asselin, *A Quebec View of Canadian Nationalism An Essay by a Dyed-in-the-Wool French-Canadian, on the best means of Ensuring the Greatness of the Canadian Fatherland,* (Montreal, 1909), pp. 11-20.

The Quebec Nationalist View

of Imperial Defence

Shall Canada contribute to the defence of Great Britain otherwise than through the defence of her own territory? And if she stays at home, to what extent is she in duty bound to defend herself?

In the consideration of this subject, one is justified in assuming that there are not several ways of contributing to the defence of the Mother Country abroad. Could anything, for instance, be more illogical than to acknowledge a military duty to the Mother Country on the part of the colonies, and at the same time reserve the right for the latter to say when, and how, the duty shall be performed? You want Canada to contribute to just wars only? But who will judge of the justness of the war? In the turmoil of passions that any war will arouse, who will seriously attempt to condemn the cause of the Mother Country and advise something that might tend to weaken it? The manner in which the South African contest, bitterly condemned as it was by some of England's leading men, was "ukased" out of discussion by the Canadian Press, shows the idea of such an attempt to be preposterous. Viewed in the light of that precedent, Sir Wilfrid Laurier's proposal, that the sending of Canadian ships out of Canadian waters be subjected to the consent of Parliament, will not bear examination. The action must be lightning-like, or it will be useless. And, supposing the Colonials to be unanimously opposed to the war, and sensible enough, and strong-minded enough to assert their opposition, would not that repudiation be such a blow to England as no subsequent contribution, however heavy, could make up for? There is hardly more sense in the cash contribution proposal, unless the contribution is based on the principle of obligation and the quota determined accordingly. And here again, once the principle admitted, you must go at it manfully, and take up the burden in no niggardly spirit. The Quebec Nationalist, for fear of the consequences, will not admit the principle.

It is said, in support of the principle of contribution, that the Canadian taxpayer should be ashamed to put up 50 cents a year for the defence of the Empire, when the British-Islander is assessed to the tune of $3.50 for the Navy alone. When you stop to think of it, this sort of argument seems almost too silly to be reasoned about. If you live in a backwoods country, you will have to pay heavier freight charges than the city dweller for your groceries. If in a city, you will have to pay higher water rates and higher rentals than the backwoodsman. Likewise, if the very existence of your country depends on Maritime trade, you must be prepared to make the expenditure which the protection of that trade will entail. When the British-Islander asks Canada to assist in ensuring him low rates of transportation for the foodstuffs he needs and the manufactured goods he has

to sell, would not Canada be justified in filing a counter-claim for the excess of cost involved in three thousand miles of land transportation through a sparsely settled country? Three dollars and fifty cents per head is comparatively not a large sum for a country in the geographical situation of England; and it is a fair subject of debate whether the unquestionable weight of it on the shoulders of the Briton to-day is not primarily due to an iniquitous land system by which a privileged few are allowed, directly or indirectly, to squeeze $750,000,000 a year from the people, and for which those "blawsted" Colonials are not responsible to the extent of one penny. At any rate, when called upon to assess herself for the protection of her sea-commerce, Canada may well ask who would be the chief beneficiary of that protection. The latest Year Book will show that the sea-going shipping entered and cleared at Canadian ports is in round figures one seventh Canadian, two sevenths Foreign and four sevenths British, and that, leaving out the coasting vessels, whose work could be done by the railroads in war time, Canada's share is almost reduced to a vanishing point. Neutral ships not being liable to seizure unless carrying contraband of war, it is virtually the English hulls and bottoms, engaged in Canadian trade for the personal gain of the English shipper, that Canada is asked to protect. Canada, with all her ports blockaded, could do all her shipping through American ports without permanent injury to her commercial interests. Our refusal to pay the piper for the English trader is certainly a matter-of-fact policy, but what of the English trader's refusal to meet his obligations?

Nor do we, the Quebec Nationalists, agree that Canada should increase her present contribution if she in any way

added to Great Britain's liabilities; for the question would then arise whether our present status is more burdensome to the Mother Country than it is to us, or, to put it otherwise, whether, for Canada, the benefits of Colonialism are greater than its drawbacks. To answer this question in the negative, one need not have read Mr. John S. Ewart's political Essays, nor stick to the old-time view of England's rôle in the treaty negotiations with the United States regarding Canada. Some of the disadvantages pointed out by Mr. Ewart are indeed trifling. We will also admit that England, considering the position she had put us in by the treaty of Paris at the close of the American War, did her best in the subsequent boundary arrangements. Still, it must be owned that the danger of foreign, and more especially of American aggression, is augmented rather than diminished by our Colonial state. With her tremendous work of internal development ahead of her, Canada has no more business outside her own territory than Argentina or Brazil. The chances of her coming in conflict with foreign powers on the high roads of the world are, for a century to come, reduced to a minimum in so far as she is personally concerned. As a British colony, the hand of all of England's enemies is raised against her. It was our connection with England that brought about the invasion of Canada in 1775 and in 1812, and put us on the brink of war in 1866; . . . It is for the sake of England that we are called upon to defend ourselves against Germany, a nation we have no motives of our own to hate, and still less to fight. Canada cannot take part in Great Britain's treaty arrangements unless, viewing herself as an integral part of that country,—which she is not,—she agrees to be represented at Westminster, and, by reason of her lesser strength, submits her-

self in advance to any decisions that the majority may take in her name. And, as long as England makes treaties for herself and possessions, she will not care for our interests more than she did when she allied herself with Japan and thereby put us at the mercy of the American people in the event of war between Japan and this latter nation. England did not look beyond the narrow range of her own interests, when, at The Hague, she helped to vote down the proposed immunity of merchant ships from seizure, which would have insured the safety of Canada's sea commerce without armaments.

It is all very well to speak of the additional armaments required by Britain for the defence of her colonies, but if you pretend that the colonies are practically valueless to the Mother Country, and, therefore, that the loss of them would not injure her, you might as well reckon that in all wars which Canada's interests did not determine, every blow aimed at the colony is so much hitting and so much blood and money saved the Mother Country.

Of course, Canada is not valueless to Great Britain. Indeed, the most rabid Imperialist would not dare assert anything of the kind. This country's railways bring the head and heart of the British military system three weeks nearer the Pacific Ocean, and they are bound to get a new strategic value from the building of the all-American Panama canal. Our harbors would be splendid bases of supplies in a contest with the States. The monopoly of our nickel ore would give Britain an advantage over all the other powers except France for the making of armor-plate. Our coal deposits she could draw upon at will. Our Finance Ministers will continue to pay to the British investor one half to one per cent more on his money than he

could get on any safe European market, or than we could get money for on the French market; and sentiment will not always be excluded from such transactions. What is represented as philanthropy on the part of the British capitalist towards our railway and industrial ventures, looks like a search for good investments in a land of promise, where social disturbances and anti-Capitalistic legislation, the nightmare of moneyed classes throughout Europe, are not yet to be feared. The British manufacturer may always expect from our government the best terms consistent with our own industrial growth. Half the moral prestige of the Mother Country in the affairs of the world rests on the extent of her colonies, irrespective of any levies of men and money which she may be permitted to make on them. It was only yesterday that Lord Dundonald represented the wholesale emigration of British paupers to the colonies as the cure for the present social discontent. But all this only serves to bring home the absurdity of that talk about our unfulfilled duty to the new-fangled and ill-defined "Empire". . . .

Some will ask if Nationhood would not, in the end, be more costly than the proposed contribution, and this may at first glance appear like a hard nut to crack. For myself, I have, in a previous work, endeavored to point out a number of ways in which a Canadian nation of eight or ten million people—not to speak of the twenty-year distant twenty millions —could hold her own very respectably in the race of nations. The Monroe Doctrine must be taken as a fact, not a theory. It is no more unbecoming in us to trust to its protection than for any of the smaller powers of Europe, like Belgium, Holland, Bulgaria and Switzerland, to shield themselves behind the conflicting

interests of their big neighbors. England herself, by withdrawing her North Atlantic fleet from Canadian waters, thrust us into the care of our neighbors as far as European aggression went. Germany's aggressiveness in South America would call for a much larger British force in South American waters, but for the American policy of exclusion. And Monroe's principle will be a greater safeguard to us against European or Asiatic hostilities than even the armed strength of England. In the United States we can have no faith. The amiable Nation of Pirates which stole Texas, Cuba, Porto-Rico and the Philippines, cannot be depended on to act justly towards a weaker nation. But if you own that England would not go to war with the Americans for our sake,—and this seems more unlikely than ever,— how can you pretend that the national status would more fatally bring us under the American hegemony? Twelve years ago, the United States only had their negro problem to cope with. Since then, they have put a finger in the Porto-Rican pie, and another in the Philippine pudding. They have become a World Power, and assumed the responsibilities of a World Power. A combination could be made against them with the South American Republics. Alliances or ententes could be made against them with European or Asiatic powers needing our transportation facilities or our commercial favors. Canada could secure a moral advantage over them by agreeing to submit all differences to international arbitration. She could derive additional security by making military training compulsory in the schools and recasting her militia on the Swiss pattern. These are only a few of the means by which she could make herself as strong with fifteen or twenty million people as the United States with their hundred millions. This, however, is misplacing the question. If we are expected, under the proposed Imperial Defence system, to shoulder all the liabilities of Nationhood, why should we continue to drag the fetters of Colonialism? Why should we not, in our external relations, look for that consideration which is the lot of all independent states however small, and let that proud spirit which the full enjoyment of Nationhood can alone beget, impel us to great deeds? That, and nothing else, is the question.

Part III

Reflections on a Theme

In some respects the interpretations of the imperialist-nationalist conflict are really continuations of the debate inaugurated in the late nineteenth century. Historians have not only looked at different aspects of this clash, they have also asked different questions from within different frames of reference. Naturally they have arrived at dissimilar impressions of what imperialism and nationalism meant. Some of the following selections do not even mention the personalities whose views were given in the first two parts of this collection, but the central issues which they raise are really much the same.

O. D. Skelton was one of the leading exponents of the liberal nationalist approach to Canadian history. Born in 1878, he had taught political economy at Queen's, and, from 1925 to 1941, was under-secretary of state for external affairs. The conflict between nationalism and imperialism was the central theme of many of his books, particularly his classic, *The Life and Letters of Sir Wilfrid Laurier* (1921). Skelton saw Canadian history as the gradual, almost inevitable, and certainly irreversible progress from colonial subordination to self-government, and his works were in large part devoted to elucidating and chronicling the political decisions and the establishment of precedents which marked this process. His interpretation of imperialism was, in some respects, ambiguous. He recognized that Canadian imperialism did embody a "spirit of nationalism" and he conceded that the policy of imperial co-operation—"the policy whereby each great colony became independent of outside control but voluntarily acted in concert with the mother country and sister states on matters of common concern"— was an advance over simple colonial status. Yet he was also convinced that by the first decade of this century imperialism had become a threat to the very sense of national-

ism it had helped to foster and that it was dangerous to national unity. In the 1920's Skelton, like most Canadians, placed more emphasis upon freedom from outside control than upon acting "in concert."

Like Skelton, and John Ewart, whose concept of nationalism is explained here by David M. L. Farr of Carleton University, Frank H. Underhill accepted the leading tenets of isolationism. From 1927 to 1955 a professor of history in the University of Toronto, he was one of the founders of the Co-operative Commonwealth Federation in 1932 and an inveterate commentator upon Canadian politics. Underhill dismissed traditional Canadian fears of the United States as foolish and held that the British connection had been one of the chief sources of both the Canadian inferiority complex and the lack of an exciting reform tradition. The Union Jack, he once remarked, should be made of wool so that it would shrink along with the Empire. Underhill was one of the few historians to devote much attention to Canadian intellectual history and in a series of lecures on the CBC in 1963 he attempted to set out the different ways in which Canadians have thought about Canada. These reflections are interesting not only for the perceptive comments upon the imperialists and nationalists but also because in 1963 Underhill was in fact evaluating some of his own earlier convictions.

What separates the concluding selections by N. Penlington and D. G. Creighton from the approach typified by Underhill and Skelton is much more than a difference in subjects. Noted for his celebrated biography of Sir John A. Macdonald and his *Commercial Empire of the St. Lawrence* (1937), in which he demonstrated that the St. Lawrence river system was the ancestor of modern Canada, Creighton has taught at the University of Toronto since 1927. In his

lecture on the renewed relevance of Macdonald for Canadians of the 1950's he described the major devices of the nation building programme—the transcontinental railway, western development, and central Canadian industrialization—and emphasized that the British connection, the national alliance, was fundamental to Canadian existence. Though his remarks apply to Macdonald they might also be taken to apply by implication to those imperialists who also hoped for what they frequently termed an alliance and who, as Professor Norman Penlington of Michigan State University makes clear, identified imperial unity with Canadian survival—against American pressure. Macdonald had attended the founding meeting of the Imperial Federation League, and he once said that he was in complete agreement with the line of argument presented in Parkin's essay "The Reorganization of the British Empire." Like many Canadian imperialists he dismissed plans for any kind of legislative union of the Empire, but saw little conflict between the furthering of Canadian autonomy and transforming the Empire in due time into an alliance of equals. In a sense what happened to Macdonald's design was also the fate that overtook imperialism. But what is especially noteworthy about these reflections is that the estimate and meaning one attaches to imperialism, and the general state of mind it represented, still very much depend upon how one looks at Canada, her relations with the United States and her outlook to the outside world. The historian A. R. M. Lower has recently reminded us that Canada is a country whose fundamental problems are never solved. Since imperialism and nationalism raised many of these perpetual Canadian questions it is hardly surprising that these forces should be interpreted so differently.

Oscar Douglas Skelton, *Life and Letters of Sir Wilfrid Laurier,* (Toronto, Oxford University Press, Toronto, 1921), Vol. II, pp. 60-65. Reprinted by permission of the literary executors of the estate of O. D. Skelton, Mr. H. H. Skelton, and Mrs. A. R. Menzies, and of the Carleton Library Series.

The Liberal Nationalist

Overview

The new imperialist movement was not peculiar to Britain or to Canada. The whole white world was well in the grip of a passion for expansion, an absorption in *welt-politik,* a scramble for prestige and profit, which was to sweep it on to bankruptcy and chaos. The hopes of world peace and economic harmony men had entertained in the brief interlude of sanity in the sixties, had been shattered and laughed to scorn. National rivalry was yearly growing more intense. The spirit of nationalism drove subject peoples to seek freedom, defeated states to regain their lost provinces, and free and successful nations to find fresh fields for the pride and energy developed in their struggle. Nationalism went to seed in imperialism. It offered a sanction for protectionism at home and economic exploitation abroad. It provided a stimulus to the growth of armaments, needed to protect each state from its neighbours, and confirming in their growth military castes and armament cliques; the dominance Germany enjoyed in Europe after the victory of its efficient military machine over Austria and France, the weight which her invincible navy gave Britain in the councils of the world, stirred emulation. The consolidation of the great states of Europe, attained after centuries of struggle, set them free to join in the scramble for overseas possessions in which for a century Britain had had no competitor. In Africa and Asia and the isles of the sea—with America barred by the Monroe Doctrine—great states and some of the small made haste to stake out fields for exploitation. In the crowded years since 1880 Germany had appropriated a million miles, Portugal and Belgium, or her monarch, each nearly as much, and France more than all three, while Russia rolled remorselessly across Asiatic plains, and even the United States was soon to enter on its career of Philippine expansion and Caribbean imperialism.

It is not surprising that Britain shared in this movement. She entered it more slowly; satiated with world-wide possessions, experienced in the drawbacks and delusions of empire, checked by vigorous and independent criticism at home, her statesmen never annexed more than their next neighbour's lands, a trifle, in these fifteen years, of some two and a half million miles, ranging from Nigeria to New Guinea. But steadily, as African hinterlands overlapped and states crowded together, as competition in the world's markets grew keener and British trade failed to advance, as the jostling of newer rivals, the preaching of professor and poet dervishes of Anglo-Saxondom, the Seeleys and the Kiplings, left their mark, the British people were stirred to a more aggressive and more conscious share in the race. The decline and defeat of the Liberal party and Liberal opinions was one manifestation of the new tendency; it had been

the Liberal policy of granting self-government which had held the white empire together, but Liberalism had little in common with this new expansion in tropical lands and among subject peoples. Still more significant was the decision of Joseph Chamberlain, the most forceful character in British politics, on the formation of the new Unionist government of Lord Salisbury in 1895, to choose the hitherto secondary and routine post of Secretary of the Colonies.

As Disraeli had typified the imperialism against which Gladstone had fought, the imperialism which strutted in European council chambers and Indian pageants and cared little for kinsmen overseas or markets for surplus goods, so Chamberlain personified the newer imperialism with its emphasis on the sublime virtues of the Anglo-Saxon, its reviving interest in the Englishman overseas, its assumption of a mission toward the darker races, and its keenness for new markets. Mr. Chamberlain's imperialism was narrowly racial; there was no room in his empire for Frenchmen or Dutchmen save as they were transformed into Englishmen, while the lesser breeds of Africa and Asia must accept the rule of their trustees for all time: he glorified the Anglo-Saxon race,—"that proud, persistent, self-asserting and resolute stock," he declared in Toronto in 1887 on his way to the fisheries arbitration at Washington, "that no change of climate or condition can alter, and which is infallibly destined to be the predominating force in the future history and civilization of the world. . . . I am an Englishman. I refuse to make any distinction between the interests of Englishmen in England, in Canada, and in the United States." His other dominating conviction was the need of securing markets overseas if

England was to hold her place and her prosperity. . . .

In Canada it seemed that the new imperialism was to find full acceptance and justification. The desire for closer imperial unity had greatly strengthened during the nineties. Among English-speaking Canadians pride of race was strong, pride in the unchallenged might of England's navy, pride in the valour and efficiency of her army, pride in the justice and firmness which had marked her foreign policy, pride in the honour and capacity of her Gladstones and Salisburys. The long reign of Queen Victoria had furnished imperial sentiment a rallying-point; her domestic virtues, her sorrows, her womanly sympathies, the reflected glories of the Victorian era, and, perhaps not least, the linking of her name with the happiest holiday of all the year, the climax day of springtime, had given her portrait the post of honour in hundreds of thousands of Canadian homes; distance, and the dazzling light that surrounds a throne, had concealed her weaknesses, her persistent and futile efforts to restore the personal control of the sovereign, her jingoism, her dynastic and pro-German view of European politics, and had left the legend of perfection unquestioned. A natural resentment against the aggressive and unneighbourly policy of the United States had strengthened imperial feeling; traditions of the sufferings and the heroism of the United Empire Loyalists were still fresh in many minds, there were still Canadians who were fighting the battles of 1812, and the Venezuela message of Secretary Olney and the prohibitive Dingly tariff played into their hands. Not least important, was the effect of reviving prosperity and confidence, in making Canadians feel they must take a more active and independent part in the world,

and must cease to be a colony. It was really a spirit of nationalism that was stirring, but for a time it took the channel of imperialism. Imperial partnership might be a permanent ideal, or it might be only a step toward nationhood, but in any case it represented a distinct advance over colonialism.

As the imperialism of these days was distinctly racial, it was not surprising that the French-Canadian population did not enter into it with enthusiasm. It has already been observed that the politicians foremost in advocacy of imperial federation were foremost also in the attempt to anglicize Canada, to narrow the use of the French tongue,—the McCarthys, the McNeills, the Tyrwhitts, the Wallaces. To expect active enthusiasm for an Anglo-Saxon empire was absurd. Here and there a French-Canadian public man, notably Israel Tarte, had joined the Imperial Federation League, but the great body

stood aloof. With their own mother country, France, they had little contact; immigration had ceased two centuries before, the France of revolutions and anti-clericalism was not the France of old, and the Church had combined with the British government to cut off intercourse with this dangerous land. French-Canadians could not escape from passive colonialism by the road that was being taken by the English-speaking Canadians, and the way of nationalism was not yet open. These oldest sons of Canada could not become Anglo-Saxon, they did not want to become French, they were not encouraged to become Canadian, and so they remained for the present *Québecquois* and *Canadiens*. . . .

. . . Only in an independent Canada could the full equality of the two races be attained which was indispensable for lasting unity.

Frank H. Underhill, *The Image of Confederation The Massey Lectures Third Series* (Toronto, Canadian Broadcasting Corporation, 1964), pp. 27-33, 35-41, 43-45. Reprinted by permission of the Canadian Broadcasting Corporation, © 1964.

History against Geography,

Imperialism against

Isolationism

. . . The late eighties and early nineties mark the point when our national self-confidence reached its lowest level. "We have come to a period in the history of this young country" wrote Wilfrid Laurier to Edward Blake "when premature dissolution seems to be at hand. What will be the outcome? How long can the present fabric last? Can it last at all? All these are questions which surge in my mind and to which dismal answers suggest themselves." There must have been a good many conversations along these lines in those days.

Out of this situation emerged a movement in 1887 for Commercial Union with the United States. The controversy that went on for the next five or six years raised deeper questions about the nature of the Canadian identity than Canadians had yet faced. . . .

Let me go back to Goldwin Smith. His book on *Canada and the Canadian Question* of 1891 is the most pessimistic book that has ever been written about Canada, and he advanced the most radical

solution for the frustrations of the day—union with the United States. . . .

To Smith, . . . , the United States represented the quintessence of everything he admired in English society and civilization, purified of all the elements he detested. The hope of democracy in the English-speaking world rested upon the United States. This was why he dreamed of a reunion of the two separated branches of the race, and why he saw the union of Canada and the States as a possible first step towards this broader reunion. No doubt, he had some dreams that his own function in history would be to take a leading part in the achievement of this "moral federation of the English-speaking peoples", as he called it.

Note that French-speaking Quebec had no part to play in these dreams. The Catholic, ultramontane theocracy of Quebec was simply an obstacle in Canada to the progress of modern, liberal, democratic civilization. Smith never seemed to realize in the 1880s that Leo XIII had succeeded Pius IX in the Vatican. "Science and democracy" as he put it "do not go to Canossa." He failed to foresee the growth of Catholicism in America as a whole. It was Puritan America, as it had been Puritan England, that was his ideal.

Smith had also, while still an English citizen, made a name for himself by his outspoken views on the British Empire. We need to understand this Manchester philosophy of his if we are to appreciate why he was so certain that Canada could not remain indefinitely a British dependency. Here I quote from a book of his, *The Empire*, which he published before he left England:

We are keeping the colonies in a perpetual state of political infancy, and **preventing**

the gristle of their frame from being matured and hardened into bone . . . We have given them all that we really have to give —our national character, our commercial energy, our aptitude for law and government, our language. We have given them the essence of our constitution . . . The accidents of that constitution—the relics of the feudal world in which it was wrought—we can no more give them than we can give them our history or our skies. England is a European aristocracy, Canada is an American democracy . . . I am no more against colonies than I am against the solar system, I am against dependencies when nations are fit to be independent . . . But grant that Canada cannot stand as a nation by herself, it is with a nation in America, not with a nation in Europe, that she must ultimately blend . . . And while she remains a province, Canada is, in fact, blending insensibly with the United States . . . There is but one way to make Canada impregnable, and that is to fence her round with the majesty of an independent nation.

Smith had the early nineteenth-century, romantic, mystic faith in the miracle-working powers of nationhood. When, after experience in Canada, he decided that we had not the capacity for nationhood on our own, there was no other destiny for us than absorption into the great American nation that was the hope of democracy. . . .

The best answers to the Goldwin Smith thesis about the destiny of Canada came from two Maritimers: George M. Grant, Nova Scotian by birth, then Principal of Queen's University; and George R. Parkin, a New Brunswicker, and a missionary for the cause of imperial federation, for which Grant was also an enthusiastic preacher. It has struck me how often the best exponents of the imperial idea in Canada have come from the Maritime provinces: men such as Grant

and Parkin among intellectuals; such as Howe, Tupper, Foster, Beaverbrook, among the men of affairs. Whatever careers some of them may have had in the larger Canada, Canada as such seems to have failed to answer to some deep emotional demand of their natures. Here in Ontario, our imperialists may have felt equally impassioned—they certainly expressed themselves vehemently enough—but one gets the impression about so many of them that a good deal of the attraction of the British connection to them has been its function as a status-symbol. It marks them off from mere French-Canadians who suffer from the misfortune of lacking a British mother-country, and from mere working-class or agrarian radicals whose zeal for narrow domestic causes shows that they have never mixed with the English governing classes.

Grant was an enthusiastic Canadian as well as an imperialist. He had accompanied his friend, the engineer Sandford Fleming, across Canada on the expedition that explored the Yellowhead route through the sea of mountains to the Pacific, and he was thrilled by the potentialities of his country. The challenge of difficulties only roused him to greater energy; these difficulties were only the growing pains in our history. His objections to Smith's ideas were temperamental almost as much as intellectual. His real objection was that Smith in his cold rational analysis paid no attention to all the traditions and sentiments that had grown up in our Canadian past:

They (Canadians) feel that he is ignorant of the deepest feelings of Canadians . . . As an Englishman and an Oxford man, Goldwin Smith is incapable of understanding Canadian sentiment . . . Before knowing Canada he made up his mind what Canadian

sentiment ought to be . . . He could do such a grand work for Canada if he would only lead us in reforming what should be reformed, one step at a time, instead of insisting that the whole house be pulled down about our ears . . . I look forward to the happy reunion of our race with as much longing as Dr. Goldwin Smith, but to begin it with a second disruption is out of the question.

The best answer of all to Smith came from Parkin. Before he made his name as a propagandist for imperial federation, Parkin had been headmaster of the collegiate school in Fredericton, which he had vainly tried to persuade his community to turn into a residential school modelled on the English public schools. His object had been to train the minds and characters of young men, some of whom would in due course show themselves capable of a higher form of politics than was current in New Brunswick. Parkin and Grant and all our later imperialists have been moved by one great vision, that of raising the standards, moral and intellectual, of Canadian public life. One of the great attractions of imperial federation to them was that Canadian statesmen, by becoming partners in a wider enterprise, would acquire wider viewpoints and a more mature sense of responsibility.

Parkin's reply came in a book that he published in 1892: *Imperial Federation, the Problem of National Unity*. One word in that title reveals more than Parkin quite realized, the word 'national'. The nation of which he was thinking was the British Empire as a whole. Canadian nationality seemed to him relatively insignificant. He continuously uses the words 'nation' and 'national' to apply to the wider entity. This was implicitly a denial of the thesis on which Canadian Liberals

by the 1890s were beginning to unite, that the relations between Canada and Great Britain must be diplomatic relations between two national states and not constitutional relations within one federal state. And the Liberals, of course, had the future with them.

Parkin, however, had more than this to his argument. His main preoccupation was with defence. In his thinking here, he was a generation younger and more up to date than Goldwin Smith. He understood that the balance of power in Europe and the world was changing to the disadvantage of Britain and the empire that she guarded, and that Canada could no longer regard herself as insulated from the outer world by British protection. He might be said to have been our first geopolitician. The function of Canada, in his vision of defence, was that of a country that, possessing harbours and coal on both the Atlantic and Pacific coasts, occupied a vital strategic position in global imperial defence. Added to this, he argued, correctly, her wheat surplus would find its markets across the ocean, not in the United States. Every interest, economic as well as military, made the connection between Canada and Britain a vital one.

Parkin's vision rose to grander heights still:

If we really have faith in our own social and Christian progress as a nation; if we believe that our race . . . can be trusted better than others to use power with moderation . . . and a deep sense of moral responsibility . . . then it cannot be inconsistent with devotion to all the highest interests of humanity to wish and strive for a consolidation of British power. It is because I believe that . . . there is this strong faith in our national integrity and in the greatness

of the moral work our race has yet to do, that I anticipate that the whole weight of Christian and philanthropic sentiment will ultimately be thrown on the side of national unity . . . inasmuch as it will give us the security which is necessary for working out our great national purposes.

This on the eve of the Jamieson Raid and the Boer War! When political argument reaches religious heights in this way, one needs to beware of it. . . .

The Boer War was a great watershed in our history. While the amount of energy that we expended on it and our sacrifices of men and money were insignificant as compared with what we went through in the two great wars of 1914 and 1939, it marked a new stage in our national experience. We ceased to be a secluded, protected colony, insulated from the direct impact of world affairs by British power and diplomacy. We began to play a part in the great twentieth-century struggles of world power-politics. All the issues about our relationship to the overseas world first became acute in these years of the Boer War. . . .

This participation by Canada in an imperialist war for power on the African continent happened to coincide fairly closely in time with the Spanish-American War in which our American neighbours took their first step towards an American overseas empire. In the United States, there was a great debate about this abandonment of North American isolation, about the morality as well as the expediency of this plunging into imperialist, overseas conquests. American liberals who were distressed at the spirit of aggrandizement displayed by their country, were defeated in this debate; but it was a great debate over the moral implications of foreign policy. How immature we still

were as compared with our American neighbours was shown by the near unanimity with which English-Canadians accepted the British advance in South Africa simply because it was British.

There were critics, of whom Henri Bourassa was the most prominent. And it was soon clear that he expressed a general French-Canadian distaste for this adventure. Goldwin Smith, as an English Manchester liberal, was also opposed. Principal Grant of Queen's who had visited South Africa and seen the activities of the gold-mining crowd on the spot, was a Pro-Boer before the war, but had to agree that there was no alternative to fighting it out when once the Boers themselves precipitated armed action. Over in London, Edward Blake, late Liberal leader, who was now an Irish Nationalist M.P. in the Imperial Parliament, stood with his fellow Irishmen in opposing the war; he had been a member of the parliamentary committee that investigated the Jamieson Raid, and he knew more than did his fellow Canadians about the sordid realities of the Rhodes high-flying dreams of empire. But these were voices in the wilderness, which went largely unheeded in the great outburst of imperial enthusiasm that swept over English-Canada.

By 1899, when the Boer War came, some important changes in the Canadian outlook were taking place. The clouds caused by the long decline in world prices were lifting, and the sun of the great wheat boom was coming out. As our exports of wheat and foodstuffs to the British market came to be the dominant element in our foreign trade, it was, for the time at least, no longer necessary to dispute whether the American market represented the chief promise or the chief threat to the Canadian future. And as the clouds lifted, Canadian self-confidence

revived. Sir Wilfrid Laurier was shortly to declare that the twentieth century belonged to Canada. This renewed national vitality, seeking outlets in which to express itself, tended among English-Canadians to take the form of an urge towards imperial adventures.

The appeal of the British connection was, moreover, strong among all English-speaking Canadians, no matter to which political party they belonged. J. W. Dafoe, in his little book on Laurier, had some interesting remarks on this subject. They are interesting because, while they are critical of his fellow English-speaking Canadians, they come from a man who was to become, by 1917, one of the most determined anti-French leaders in the country:

English-speaking Canadians were more British than the British, they were more loyal than the Queen . . . Imperialism, on the sentimental side, was a glorification of the British race; it was a foreshadowing of the happy time when this governing and triumphant people would give the world the blessing of the Pax Britannica. . . It kindled their imagination; from being colonists of no account in the backwash of the world's affairs, they became integrally a part of a great imperial world-wide movement of expansion and domination; were they not of what Chamberlain called "that proud, persistent, self-asserting and resolute stock . . . which is infallibly bound to be the predominating force in the future history and civilization of the world"? Moreover it gave them a sense of their special importance here in Canada, where the population was not "homogeneous in blood, language, and religion"; it was for them, they felt, to direct policy and control events.

This racist tone, which ran all through the imperialism of Chamberlain and Kipling in Britain, naturally repelled the French-Canadians. The more this type of Anglo-Saxon nationalism became prominent in Canada, the more the two main communal groups were alienated from each other. And the more that the fervour of Anglo-Saxondom came to centre in the Conservative party, the more inevitable it was that the French-Canadians should attach themselves to the Liberals. For this reason, if for no other, the Liberal form of nationalism had the future with it. . . .

The diamond jubilee of Queen Victoria in 1897 . . . helped powerfully in the growth of imperial sentiment. Special jubilee stamps were issued, containing a map of the world that was splashed with red wherever there were British possessions, with a proud declaration at the bottom of the stamp: "We hold a greater empire than has been." Who were the "we" who held this great empire? We Canadians? Of course not. But our Postmaster-General was identifying us with the British people who did hold it. I can remember, as a small boy of some eight years, collecting these stamps eagerly. . . .

In the summer of 1898, the year between the jubilee and the war, my childhood companions and I were playing war games introduced by an American boy, a visitor in one of the homes on our street; we were capturing Havana and Manilla for the Anglo-Saxon, Protestant American forces, who were also, as I vaguely sensed, part of "that proud, persistent, self-asserting and resolute stock which is infallibly bound to be the predominating force in the future history and civilization of the world". A small boy in a little Ontario village was well prepared by 1899 to sing *Soldiers of the Queen,* that most vulgarly boastful of all imperialist war-anthems.

In 1885, Sir John Macdonald had coldly turned down the proposal to send an official Canadian force to take part in the Soudan expedition for the relief of General Gordon, though he allowed a body of boatmen to be recruited by the British authorities for service on the Nile. He pointed out to Sir Charles Tupper, who was Canadian High Commissioner in London and who was eager to seize the opportunity to advertise Canada in Britain, that Canada had no direct interest in the Nile or the Suez Canal, and that "our men and money would therefore be sacrificed to get Gladstone & Co. out of the hole they had plunged themselves into by their own imbecility". In 1899, Sir Wilfrid Laurier, if left to follow his own view of the situation, would no doubt have shown a similar detachment from South African affairs, and would have declined to make Canadian sacrifices to get Chamberlain & Co. out of the hole they had plunged themselves into by their own imbecility. But his hand was forced by the enthusiasm in English-speaking Canada for taking part in the war. He felt that his government must act on Canadian majority opinion. So the first contingent was sent off without waiting for parliamentary sanction—a momentous step in our history, which was defended by the provision in the Order-in-Council authorizing the action that declared that this step should not constitute a precedent.

Young Henri Bourassa, the rising lieutenant of Laurier, at once raised a protest. The debate between him and Laurier on what was involved in this sending of Canadian troops overseas was one of the finest that has ever taken place in our Canadian Parliament. I quote at some length from it because the issues were so important (Bourassa's protest was twofold. In the first place he associated himself with the British Liberals who opposed Chamberlain's policy. His other main point was that this was a change in the constitutional relations of mother-country and colony. Hitherto both of them had recognized that the colony's military obligations were confined to the local defence of Canada, and that the metropolitan power had the responsibility of general imperial defence):

This great display of Imperial militarism is not intended for the purpose of this war, but is being organized to give an example and warning to the world. . . If we send 2,000 men and spend $2,000,000 to fight two nations aggregating a population of 250,000 souls, how many men shall we send, and how many millions shall we expend to fight a first-class power or a coalition of powers? And it is, no doubt, to first-class powers and to possible coalitions that the lesson and the warning were intended to be given. If we judged proper to share in the teaching, it must mean that we are ready to share in the action when the time comes of applying the lesson. . . It is the starting-point of a new policy which opens a serious point of view on the future of the country. The point of view may be glorious for those who aspire after military honours . . . But it prepares a gloomy future for the farming and labouring classes of this country.

As to the no-precedent clause, he repeated what he had said in an open letter to the prime minister: "The precedent, sir, is the accomplished fact." And he quoted from utterances of Chamberlain and the Governor General to show how they had deliberately greeted the sending of the troops as a precedent for the future co-operation of Canada and Britain in war. Canada's future involvement in European militarism was being determined now.

I do not ask for independence now, nor at any period within ordinary foresight. Not that independence is not, to my mind, the most legitimate and natural aim to which any colony should tend. . . But clear propositions as to military co-operation must be laid before parliament and thoroughly discussed, and when the terms are agreed upon, a plebiscite must be taken on the question, free from all other political issues. . . I am a Liberal of the British school. I am a disciple of Burke, Fox, Bright, Gladstone, and of the other little Englanders, who made Great Britain and her possessions what they are.

He ended by moving "that . . . this House declares that it opposes any change in the political and military relations which exist at present between Canada and Great Britain, unless such change is initiated by the sovereign will of Parliament and sanctioned by the people of Canada." Note two things about this Bourassa stand. He is speaking as a Liberal who agrees with what English Liberals were saying about the moral issues of the war. How strange that English-speaking Canadian Liberals seemed so blind to this aspect of the question! He also remains still a colonist, insisting on colonial detachment from these wider imperial responsibilities. He is not yet a full Canadian nationalist demanding that Canada assume responsibility for her own defence and foreign policy.

Laurier replied that his young friend was making too much of the situation. . . . He went on:

If we had refused at that time to do what was in my judgment our imperative duty, a most dangerous agitation would have arisen . . . which would have ended in a cleavage in the population of this country upon racial lines. . . If there is anything to which I have given my political life, it is to try to promote unity, harmony, and amity, between the diverse elements of this country . . . I am fully convinced in my heart and conscience that there never was a juster war on the part of England. . . I altogether repudiate that doctrine, that we have changed the relations, civil and military, which now exist between Great Britain and Canada. . . If we were to be compelled to take part in all the wars of Great Britain, I agree with my honourable friend that, sharing the burden, we should also share the responsibility. . . But there is no occasion to examine this contingency today. . . .

Alas, what English-Canadians observed was that there were many more of them offering their lives in South Africa than of French-Canadians. The former antagonism was not buried. And what French-Canadians were to observe in the next few years was that Bourassa had been right: "The precedent, sir, is the accomplished fact." He was prophetic. By 1914, we were plunged into that greater struggle among European powers that he had foreseen. . . .

Of course this ardent aspiration for a closely organized British Empire, with Canada a full partner in it, was never to be realized. And today we seem to have reached a general acceptance by the Canadian people as a whole of a position in which the aloofness of the French-Canadians is more effectively expressed than the organic imperial unity longed for by the federationists. English-Canadians no longer insist that French-Canadians must adjust themselves to a great world-wide English-speaking empire. Out of all the controversies that filled the air from 1899 to 1945, what emerged was a Canadian nationalism that insisted on the complete national sovereignty of Canada, and that refused any economic or military schemes such as would bind us in one community

with Britain. Canada has, however, accepted responsibilities in Europe that spring from our partnership in an Atlantic alliance rather than a Britannic alliance, and responsibilities in the world at large that are undertaken as a member of the United Nations rather than of the British Commonwealth.

This development was not foreseen by any Canadian before 1919, and the logic that was driving us towards it was denied by many Canadians during the long armistice from 1919 to 1939. We have arrived at a conclusion that was beyond the categories of our thinking during most of the time we were moving towards it.

As one looks back now, it seems evident that the North American isolationists, English-Canadian and French-Canadian, were blind in their failure to see the realities of the international balance of power in this twentieth century. In 1914 and 1939, we were bound to come into the war because we could not afford to see Britain and France eliminated as great European powers. The Unit-ed States came in for the same reason, and it did not matter how much we may have disapproved certain aspects of British and French policy. Today we keep armed forces in Europe because we cannot afford to see the West European powers overrun by totalitarian invasion. This continuous policy of intervention in Europe was really all the time based on inescapable calculations of power politics and not on a sentimental attachment to Britain.

Today our ties with Britain have weakened, in spite of the common Crown, because Britain is no longer a great world power. It was British power that guaranteed our security in the world, acted as a counterweight against American pressures, and made it worth while for us to follow the British lead in two world wars. But now that British power has been so drastically reduced, the British connection has lost that magnetic attraction that it used to exercise over us. The power that guarantees our security now is that of the United States as leader of the Atlantic alliance. We have to contribute what we can to make that alliance effective.

David M. L. Farr, "John S. Ewart," *Our Living Tradition Second and Third Series,* ed., R. L. McDougall (Toronto, Published in association with Carleton University by University of Toronto Press, 1959), pp. 191-204. Reprinted by permission of the University of Toronto Press.

The Nationalism of

John Ewart

Ewart produced his first essay on the constitutional destiny of Canada in 1904. It was a period when the possibilities of a separate Canadian existence were being more widely appreciated. Constitutionally, many bars remained to its realization. Canadian autonomy in domestic matters was absolute, and in the field of external affairs it operated in the determination of trade relations. But political relations—foreign policy as such—still lay beyond the control of the Canadian government. The Dominion had recently been aroused by the controversial Alaska Boundary award, which had been popularly interpreted to mean that Canada's inability to control her foreign relations would inevitably result in a sacrifice of national interests. Thus the prevailing mood of confidence in 1904—the feeling that the twentieth century belonged to Canada—was tempered by the impression that changes would have to be made in the control of Canada's foreign relations.

But to what end should changes be directed? This was the subject of a debate into which Ewart plunged with enthusiasm. He took the view that the promise of Canadian nationhood, "the strong strivings of strenuous manhood," as he put it, dictated no other course than that Canada should assume full control over her external policy. This solution, which appears so reasonable to us in 1959, seemed wild and chimerical to English Canadians in 1904. The prevailing opinion among those who thought about Canada's relations with the outside world was concerned with exploring the possibilities of a common foreign policy for Canada and Great Britain, a policy in which the smaller country should have some influence and agree to bear some responsibility. This view had been held by a whole generation of English Canadians, from Colonel Denison and D'Alton McCarthy in the eighties to Stephen Leacock and W. L. Grant in the years before the First World War.

Essentially the conflict between Ewart and those who believed in the consolidation of the British Empire revolved around the interpretation of the objective —nationalism. Each group started from the same premise: that the colonial status was a "worn-out, by-gone thing," to use Leacock's phrase. To continue it was to destroy the self-respect of the Canadian people. Nationalism to Ewart meant the separate "Kingdom of Canada"—Canada, "self-existent, autonomous, sovereign." His opponents thought of a national life encompassing the entire British Empire, a sort of integral nationalism based largely on race. This was the viewpoint of Lord Milner, whom Ewart came to regard as the arch-enemy of Canadian hopes. Milner was convinced that Great Britain could not survive in the competitive twentieth century without a close connection with the other regions peopled by

British stock. "It seems unnatural to me . . . to lose interest in and attachment to my fellow countrymen because they settle across the sea. It is not the soil of England . . . which is essential to arouse my patriotism, but the speech, the traditions, the spiritual heritage, the principles, the aspirations of the British race. They do not cease to be mine because they are transplanted—my horizon must widen, that is all." The historically minded will hear in this twentieth-century debate echoes of the great controversy that had disrupted the British Empire 150 years before. At the time of the American Revolution Englishmen like Lord Mansfield and American Tories like Governor Hutchinson had also interpreted the British Empire as one nationality, while Americans like Jefferson and Adams had felt that the interests of the colonies were distinct and deserving of individual recognition. In the 1770's, as well as in the early 1900's, the latter views were regarded as subversive of the British connection.

Ewart's political thought rang the changes on a single basic idea—nationalism as the destiny of Canada. Nationalism was incompatible with the existing colonial status. "Physically and mentally Canadians are strong, sturdy and fibrous. Politically they are faint, frail and spineless. I would have them hold up their heads." And again: "An American gets more respect in London than a colonist. In my opinion, he is entitled to it." In the face of centrifugal tendencies there was an urgency in proclaiming Canadian nationalism. Unity was precarious because of "our geographical separations, our racial divisions; our polyglot immigration, the closer natural associations of our west with the United States rather than with our east. We need some stronger solidifying influence than three lines of railways and a national debt." With nationhood declared, the attributes would follow.

Yet Ewart did not disparage the advances that had already been made in securing freedom of action for Canada. It was to safeguard these gains that he supported so vigorously Sir Wilfrid Laurier's stand at successive Imperial Conferences from 1897 to 1911. Joseph Chamberlain's plans for the strengthening of imperial unity, whether by political, military, or economic means, seemed to him, as to Laurier, to point to the submission of Canada to a governance not her own. His attack on the various schemes of imperial federation that were presented during the Chamberlain period was characteristic—he asked for definition. This was a shrewd stroke, for it laid bare the fatal flaw in all the movements for consolidation: the failure of their adherents to agree on concrete proposals. The sole concession which Ewart was prepared to make to the concept of unity was a grudging approval of the schemes—Fleming's Pacific cable, Mulock's imperial penny postage—for improving Empire communications. These projects represented a functional approach to the problem; they were imperialism "of the practical Canadian sort." One concludes that Ewart was commending what was to become a familiar type of Canadian contribution to international affairs—that of the engineer. The Colombo Plan and International Civil Aviation Organization, for instance, differ in degree, not in conception, from the Pacific cable scheme.

"Canada must some day have something to say upon the greatest of all national questions—the question of peace and war." Ewart said this in 1907. Over the next few years he devoted some of his most penetrating writing to the subject.

Nothing illustrates the strong points of his method better than this discussion: the unwavering insistence upon the primacy of the national objectives of Canada, the ability to cut through legal traditionalism to the heart of the question, the lucid marshalling of the evidence. Even today the subject of the war relationship with Great Britain is an extraordinarily difficult one for Canadians to assess, as the furore over the Suez crisis proved. In 1912, with Canada just emerging onto the world stage and the ties of sentiment more compelling than they are today, it was terrifyingly formidable.

Basically the problem arose from the incongruity of Canada's position as a self-governing colony within the British Empire. Legally it was clear that when Great Britain was at war her colonies were at war also, yet the South African War had demonstrated, and Laurier had repeatedly stated, that Canada claimed the right to determine the extent of her participation in any British war. Much thought had been devoted to the question of devising machinery for the joint control of foreign policy and the sharing of the burdens of imperial defence, yet Ewart was convinced that there was nothing pertinent to Canadian interests in these efforts. Not only was a joint foreign policy impracticable for autonomous states with separate executives and legislatures, but Great Britain's security was only indirectly the security of Canada. Canada's safety lay, rather, in her geographical position on the North American continent. This was the outstanding fact which should influence all Canadian foreign policy. Canada and the United States formed a natural defensive aggregation, he argued. There was "nothing humiliating in [this] community of military interest with the United States"; the humiliating aspect was in not

being free to affirm it through a treaty of mutual guarantee with the Americans. . . .

The imperative need was to define the relationship with Great Britain before defence arrangements were consummated. Canada must approach this problem free from the enthusiasms of emotion. British motives should be viewed in a clear light. ". . . Britain planted colonies (calling them plantations) for the same reason that a farmer plants cabbages—because of their benefit to himself; and Britain protected her plantations for the same reason that the farmer protected his—because he wanted them for himself." From this the conclusion followed that Canada was under no obligation, legal or political, to participate in British wars. Her policy should be to enter into alliances with countries who could assist her, for specific objectives and under specific conditions. In practice, as far as the relationship with Great Britain was concerned, the Ewart approach might mean Canadian neutrality in a British war, depending on the circumstances of the case and their relation to Canadian interests.

A limited alliance for war was but one of Ewart's suggestions for future association with Great Britain; more important was his conception of the constitutional relationship. Here he showed himself not so much as an innovator as an inheritor of an important national tradition. His view was that the relationship should be that of a personal union, a union under a common crown. "The King's Canadian ministers shall advise him upon all things Canadian, with the same constitutional authority as British ministers advise their Sovereign upon all things British." To describe succinctly this new position Ewart suggested the use of the phrase "Kingdom of Canada," returning to the original designation proposed

by Sir John A. Macdonald in 1867. In Ewart's eyes, Macdonald, tested by his actions and not by his speeches, was the great architect of Canadian nationhood. He chided his countrymen for a failure to acknowledge Macdonald's vision. "A great many Canadians in 1911 would be afraid of Sir John's splendid Canadianism of forty-five years ago." Macdonald and those who followed his mode of thought were thus the inspiration for Ewart's "king-union" concept. The list is an impressive one: Lord Monck, with his plea that Canadian Privy Councillors be granted the same style as their English counterparts; Lord Dufferin and his proposal that Canada be transformed into a "Vice-royalty"; Edward Blake stressing constitutional advance to accompany the "cultivation of a national spirit"; Laurier himself in the twentieth century.

Ewart felt that the personal union relationship, which was capable of being understood by lawyers and constitutional authorities, possessed the special merit of the precedent of the famous union between Great Britain and Hanover from 1714 to 1837. Unfortunately for Ewart's advocacy it proved difficult to explain the relationship, even to lawyers. Inevitably the question arose, did this not mean separation from Great Britain? All Canadians, Ewart would reply, "are separatists with regard to the Colonial Office and unionists in respect of the Crown." Under a personal union, the legal status of Canada would conform to the reality of her position; the *de facto* relationship would become the *de jure*. But, almost to his death, the hesitations continued.

The First World War marked an abrupt break in the course of Ewart's thought, just as it did in the life of his country. The issues of war aid and future relations were now sharpened by the urgencies of combat; constitutional advance was accelerated by the revolutionary impact of war. The years 1914-18 provide an opportunity to compare Ewart's position, as the most thoroughgoing English-Canadian nationalist of the time, with that of the unchallenged leader of French-Canadian nationality, Henri Bourassa.

Since Bourassa is one of the most misunderstood Canadians of our day it is necessary to point out at the beginning that fundamentally his views on the future of Canada differed little from Ewart's. In fact, the two men, in the pre-1914 period, may be regarded as the two sides of the same Canadian nationalist coin. To Bourassa, Ewart was "our English interpreter of nationalism" and Ewart returned the compliment with his warm welcome for Bourassa's newspapers, the *Ligue nationaliste* (1903) and *Le Devoir* (1910). Both men believed in the racial duality of Canadian nationalism and stressed the importance of mutual respect between the races in the *sine qua non* of Canadian existence. Both Ewart and Bourassa, anchored firmly to their North American setting, were suspicious of Canadian commitments abroad and sceptical of the machinations of European diplomacy. Bourassa, indeed, distinguished an aggressive, land-grabbing imperialism at the basis of British policy. This imperialism, by requiring military contributions from the colonies, as in the South African War, imperilled Canadian autonomy. Ewart, with a better understanding of the British character, did not see the danger in such extreme terms. Both men, however, reached the same conclusions: that Canada must be allowed to shape a distinctive foreign policy, free from any subordination to overseas interests.

With the outbreak of war in August,

1914, Ewart and Bourassa supported Canadian participation. Their reasons were the same: a recognition that Canada, as an Anglo-French nation, was warmly sympathetic to the plight of the parent countries in Europe. Ewart felt that Canadian aid, sent voluntarily and not from a sense of duty, represented a step towards independence. He took his place on recruiting platforms and, unlike Bourassa, tried to avoid controversial statements that would impair national unity. For this reason he discontinued the publication of *The Kingdom Papers* at the outbreak of the war.

The steady deterioration in relations between English- and French-speaking Canadians which the war produced is graphically illustrated by the record of Ewart's friendship with Bourassa. Even their deeply held and shared faith in Canada was not sufficient to overcome the lack of confidence which became apparent between Quebec and the rest of the Dominion after 1916. The increasingly racial basis of Bourassa's agitation, with its appeal to exclusiveness and grievance, seemed to Ewart to represent a deliberate challenge to Canadian national unity. Although he held no brief for the Borden government he felt it was successfully prosecuting the war effort and that it should be left free to continue this task. However, he bitterly denounced conscription, both for its principle and for the way in which it had been applied. In the "khaki election" of 1917 he threw his support behind the Liberals. He urged Laurier not to campaign solely on an anti-conscriptionist policy, which he was confident would be ineffective, but to take the line that Canada's main contribution for the rest of the war should be to increase her capacity to produce food. (It should be remembered that the fear of food

shortages was much more intense in the closing years of the First World War than at any time in the Second.) Laurier refused to follow this advice, although two of Ewart's pamphlets were used as campaign material by the Liberals. For his efforts in helping Laurier Ewart was characterized by the Ontario press as the "Bourassa of English-speaking Canadians," a phrase which was now inappropriate but which he would have valued earlier.

His estrangement from Bourassa came in 1917. By this time the French-Canadian had come to doubt the sincerity of Great Britain's motives in entering the war and thus the sincerity of English Canada's desire to continue in the struggle. The sense of imperial solidarity, expressed in the creation of the Imperial War Cabinet and the other agencies for military and economic co-operation, seemed to Bourassa to presage an "Imperialist Revolution" (the phrase is his) which he felt it his duty to expose. Ewart was also worried about the centralizing tendencies which the war had produced, but he did not feel that they had any bearing on the necessary condition of Canadian belligerency. Certainly he did not countenance Bourassa's conclusion that, in the circumstances, Canada should withdraw from an active participation in the war. In one of the last in a long series of letters to Bourassa, Ewart put the point this way: "In my view, imperialism is a domestic question and has no relation to our attitude towards Germany. I therefore see in Sir Robert Borden's excessive imperialism not a reason for alteration of Canada's opposition to her external enemies, but a reason for attack upon the imperialists." His final proposal to Bourassa, that he consult with him to see if any modifica-

tion of the conscription measure would be acceptable to Quebec, went unanswered for some months. As far as I can determine, the correspondence and the old friendship were never resumed.

Ewart's attack on the imperialists was launched in the summer of 1917, in one of the most forthright of his essays, "The Republic of Canada." The paper was inspired by his desperation at the steady process of imperial consolidation which the war had produced. To his mind the groups in England and Canada who had never ceased to hope for imperial unity were taking advantage of the opportunity offered by the war to create a new imperial structure in which Canada would sacrifice all her gains of recent years. Proposals for pooling the resources of the Dominions for common purposes, schemes for transferring political functions to appointed administrative bureaux, plans for "continuous consultation" in foreign policy and in peace-making—all these projects, either in existence or contemplated, had "wrecked beyond repair" the reality of Canadian autonomy. The climax of Canadian political evolution had been reached just before the war and now the Dominion was rapidly travelling the road to subordination. "It is all downhill," lamented Ewart, "and we have no brakes." Behind the new movement for imperial solidarity he discerned the familiar figure of his old adversary, Milner, now a member of Lloyd George's inner War Cabinet. Perhaps it was this confrontation which impelled him to set down, at the conclusion of "The Republic of Canada," the most intemperate outburst of his career.

Imperialism is the enemy—the enemy in Europe and the enemy in Canada. Imperialism was the cause of the present war. Imperialism was the cause of the American revolution. Imperialism was the cause of the Canadian rebellions. Imperialism is the curse and scourge of the world.
And this I say to the imperialists who are pressing their crown of thorns upon the brow of the Canadian people. Crush it down. Restrict our political liberty. . . . Crush it down, I say, until it enters the bone. Repeat for us the tragedy of your Transvaal imperialism. Lord Milner is once more a dominating figure. He is the same masterful aristocrat now that he was then. He drove the Boers into a war for freedom. He is reducing Canada to shameful subjugation. He has dissipated all hope of THE KINGDOM OF CANADA. He will find, I tell him, that he has but turned us to a better, for a more secure and enduring, destiny. He, principally, is the founder of THE REPUBLIC OF CANADA.

(*The Kingdom Papers,* II, 393)

A republican status for Canada was but an aberration in Ewart's thought. Although he put it forward defiantly for a few years he returned in the early twenties to the common-king relationship and expounded it until the end of his life. The First World War, a time of upheaval and mass hysteria, had succeeded in distracting, momentarily, the integrity of one of the most incorruptible of Canadians.

The ten years after the conclusion of the First World War were a period of rapid constitutional advance for Canada. In relations with Great Britain, in the field of foreign affairs, a new pastime became popular: "I spy Dominion status." This was an activity close to Ewart's heart and he played the game as enthusiastically as any autonomist of the day. The fact that there were many who took part in the campaign during these years was immensely important; it showed the enlarging effect of the four-year agony on the Western Front on the horizons of Canada.

The problem for the post-war years was to define Canadian sovereignty in all its aspects, to remove anomalies clinging to it, and to establish the foundation of a Canadian foreign policy. In all these activities Ewart showed himself to be thoroughly at home.

The period began inauspiciously for the exponents of autonomy. The "continuous consultation" and "concerted action" of the war years were carried over into the first post-war Imperial Conferences and to the Washington Conference of 1921. Ewart railed against this concept of a common foreign policy, especially as it was voiced by Borden and Meighen at these meetings. The Chanak crisis of 1922, with its breakdown in consultation within the British Empire, seemed to Ewart to vindicate his stand completely. He turned to the congenial task of promoting the centrifugal tendencies in foreign policy which now became characteristic of the Commonwealth association.

Canada's objects in foreign policy, as he saw them, were to attain security in a manner compatible with national sovereignty. A traditional method had been through concert with Great Britain, a course which he had advocated as worthy of careful study before 1914. Now he felt that an alliance with Great Britain was no longer appropriate because of a lack of similarity in the interests of the United Kingdom and Canada. British commitments under treaties and other obligations extended around the world; towards almost all these pledges Canada felt a minimum of concern. The Treaty of Sèvres, ambiguous in its application to Canada; the abortive Anglo-American guarantee to France (to Ewart an "act of the most stupendous folly"); the Treaty of Lausanne; the Locarno Pacts: none of these agreements need bind Canada to support of British foreign policy.

But was there not a moral obligation to aid Great Britain in her diplomacy? Was it not true that Great Britain had fought in the past for the humane ideals of freedom, justice, and the protection of the weak? For this reason, should Canada not be found at her side when war threatened? Ewart was at his incisive best in demolishing this assumption. In a series of substantial essays, published in volume I of *The Independence Papers,* he traced the origins of every British war since Canada became a part of the British Empire in 1763, attempting to show that there was none, with the possible exception of the French Revolutionary-Napoleonic struggle, on which the British people could look back with any degree of satisfaction. By comparison with many other countries, British motives for going to war were wholly admirable, but they were still motives framed in terms of British self-interest and not primarily in terms of the higher ideals. Canada, therefore, should feel no obligation to engage in British wars merely because they were *British* wars. Nor should Canada feel gratitude for the advantages of British protection in the past. On a number of occasions, such as the seizure of Canadian sealers in the Bering Sea in the 1880's, Canada had failed to receive naval protection from Great Britain. On other occasions she had received British support, not for her own sake, but because British interests in North America were at stake.

That the League of Nations could guarantee Canada's independence Ewart had no confidence. He saw the League as a useful centre for discussion and education in international affairs, but as

nothing more. His hesitations regarding the League as an instrument of collective security came from his studies into the origins of war, in which he had become convinced that wars do not start from "issues in dispute" but arise from "indefinable" or "predisposing" causes. War, he once said, is caused by "reasonable dissatisfaction with existing conditions." These conditions could not be corrected by conciliation machinery set up by the League of Nations. The collective security procedures of the League were objectionable, he thought, because they worked to preserve many inequitable features embodied in present European political boundaries. . . .

His suspicion of the League made Ewart a strong supporter of Mackenzie King's policy of "no commitments in advance." As he stated in a letter to Mr. King in 1925, "no pledge as to our future action . . . should be given; . . . we should reserve perfect freedom to do as we may think right when the time for decision arrives." He was happy to observe that Arthur Meighen had by 1925 abandoned his "ready, aye ready" position of the Chanak affair. When Meighen told him in conversation, "You see I am going your way," he felt that he had scored a personal triumph.

The holding of the Imperial Conference of 1926, Ewart believed, set Canada at last firmly on the high road that would lead to full national sovereignty. This major conference, the most important since the war, spelled out, in the report of Lord Balfour's committee, current constitutional practice in the British Commonwealth. We now know that the dominating figure on this committee was the Afrikaner prime minister of the Union of South Africa, General Hertzog. In his uncompromising desire to secure a redefinition of Commonwealth relations which would assert the equality of the Dominions, Hertzog resembled Ewart. In the committee his views had to be reconciled with those of the New Zealand delegation, who favoured some gesture towards imperial solidarity. Thus the Dominions were defined as "autonomous communities within the British Empire," a declaration which Ewart thought a contradiction in terms. Yet, all things considered, he was well pleased with the report, echoing J. W. Dafoe's comment that it "opens doors that can never be shut and we can pass through them into new fields whenever we have the courage to go forward." Ewart's principal reservation about the report of the Conference concerned the familiar statement, ". . . the principles of equality and similarity, appropriate to status, do not universally extend to function." To Ewart this was begging the whole question. If equality in status did not apply to function, what did it mean? Under this definition the Dominions were comparable to "soft-nosed torpedoes":

These imitation articles are made use of in a playful practice. They look like torpedoes, and, to a certain extent, they act like torpedoes, but when they hit something and are supposed to blow it to smithereens, they do nothing because they are soft-nosed. Similarly, the Dominions look like sovereign states and, to some extent they act like sovereign states, but when they are supposed to function effectively, they simply cannot because they are but faulty imitations.

(*Toronto Star*, Feb. 17, 1927)

After 1926 the final steps in the achievement of Canadian legislative independence were taken. Ewart, now in his late seventies, waited somewhat nervously for this consummation of his hopes. "I have been rather anxious," he wrote to a

friend, "as to the success in the race between my constitution and the constitution of Canada. I was apprehensive that
I would finish before the Canadian constitution reached its climax." The remaining
limitations on Canadian sovereignty were
removed in law through the passage of the
Statute of Westminster by the British Parliament on December 11, 1931. This date,
on which Great Britain formally re-
nounced all legislative control over the
Dominions, Ewart likened to a Canadian
counterpart of a declaration of independence. Yet now that the goal had been
reached there was a sense of anti-climax.
He noted ironically that the Canadian
Parliament made no comment on the
significant occasion and that there appeared to be a lack of gratitude to the
British government which had acted so
handsomely. The final *Independence
Paper,* number 15 of volume II, appeared
in April, 1932, twenty-eight years after
the series had begun. It simply quoted the
text of the Statute of Westminster, and
added a brief valedictory. In the presence
of success, it was a time for humility.

To the final achievement, the writer is
well aware that he contributed nothing as
compared with the work of Canada's five
great Premiers—Sir John A. Macdonald, Sir
Wilfrid Laurier, Sir Robert Borden, Mr.
Mackenzie King and Mr. Bennett. But working more continuously if in more humble
way, the writer may to some extent have
helped in the development of a true Canadianism, and so made easier the work of the
leaders. He would fain believe that his labors
were not altogether without effect. And the
kind acknowledgements and congratulations
which have come to him from many of those
who had not formerly sympathised with him
seem to indicate that for such belief there is
some foundation.

(*The Independence Papers,* II, 602)

Norman Penlington, *Canada and Imperialism 1896-1899*, (Toronto, University of Toronto Press, 1965), pp. 4-8, 10-11. Reprinted by permission of the University of Toronto Press.

The Anglo-Canadian Alliance

In 1867 Canada had embarked on its career in high hope of securing a continental domain. Within four years a truncated North Atlantic state expanded to the Pacific. Canada purchased the Hudson's Bay Company lands in the West, and shortly afterwards induced the colony of British Columbia to enter the Dominion on the promise of a railroad to the East. The acquisition of this vast territory and Canada's consolidation into a national unit thus demanded the construction of expensive railways to the West and to the eastern Canadian provinces, which by 1873 included Prince Edward Island.

In prosperity, this work of nation-building went confidently forward; in depression, Canada's economic vulnerability undermined the national faith. Macdonald's solution to depression and to the growth of the Dominion was western settlement, eastern manufacturing, and a Pacific railway. Only Britain could readily supply the necessary settlers and finances. But why should Britain, the home of laissezfaire, help Canada in this national work? To overcome British objections, the Canadian Government continually proclaimed the essential identity of Canadian and British interests, that is, that the building of Canada was an imperial work. . . .

By the mid-eighties Canada found an increasingly favourable response to its requests. One result was the summoning of the first Colonial Conference of 1887, which, however, accomplished little, for Britain was as reluctant to enter into closer trade relations with the colonies as they were to enter into closer defence relations with Britain. Nevertheless the more sympathetic atmosphere for colonial interests raised the price of Canadian Pacific Railway bonds in London and enabled the Canadian Government to obtain a mail subsidy for the company's steamship line across the Pacific linking Canada to Japan and Hong Kong. It is indicative of the strength of Canada's contentions that George (later Viscount) Goschen, the Chancellor of the Exchequer, complained to Sir Charles Tupper, the Canadian High Commissioner, that he had made all the concessions in the negotiations for the subsidy. In 1887 also, the Salisbury Government supported Canada diplomatically in the fishery negotiations at Washington; in 1890 it gave what amounted to naval protection of Canadian sealing rights in the Bering Sea against the United States; and in the same year it disallowed a reciprocity treaty between Newfoundland and the United States inimical to Canadian interests.

Canada needed this support, for the late eighties and early nineties saw the deepening of the depression. National policies could not counter the emigration of Canadians to the more prosperous United States; . . . In 1887 five provincial premiers in a conference at Quebec City demanded larger subsidies and the aboli-

tion of the power of disallowance of provincial legislation. The general pessimism was made worse by the split between English and French Canadians and between Protestants and Roman Catholics over the execution of Louis Riel and over the Jesuits' Estates Act of 1889. In addition to these already perilous divisions, Canada was confronted with a graver one—the commercial union movement and its vague alternative, unrestricted reciprocity. Reciprocity recalled the economically nostalgic era of the 1850's and 1860's. In those days, perhaps, reciprocity had helped save Canada from the United States; in the 1880's it was regarded by many Canadians as a threat because of its coincidence with a strong, or at least noisy, agitation to annex Canada, and the movement provoked appeals of loyalty to Britain based on the feared political consequences of closer commercial relations.

While the new Dominion pictured itself as an important state needing assistance, Britain was responding more favourably to colonial economic importunities because of the relative weakening of its own position diplomatically, economically, and defensively. In the 1860's and 1870's, for example, Britain suffered diplomatic checks; the shock of the quick German victory over France in 1870 speeded up British army reform, and the naval scares of the 1880's and 1890's led to increases in the navy; foreign tariff walls were being raised against British goods; and the United States and Germany having settled their own internal problems by the 1870's began to compete successfully with British goods in the world market.

Britain's response to this relative decline of strength was the maintenance, consolidation, and expansion of imperial power. Exponents of imperialism looking to power as a solution of Britain's problems opposed the Gladstonian solution of freedom. They preferred, for example, the maintenance of the Transvaal, not in its state of qualified freedom, but as a dependency, and they opposed Home Rule for Ireland. But to Britain's rivals, the most spectacular aspect of British imperialism was not the consolidation, but the expansion of the Empire in Africa, Asia, and the South Seas. In the 1880's, political, strategic, and economic interests largely explain particular annexations. In the 1890's, democratic imperialism played a large part, for that decade saw the British masses, made politically conscious by the vote, mass education, and an interest in their own economic and social welfare, exercising an increasing political influence. The power of democratic imperialism was further intensified by jingoism—mass xenophobia—in the late nineties by, for example, the demonstration of naval might at the Diamond Jubilee, the victory of Kitchener at Omdurman over the dervishes, and the humiliation of France at Fashoda.

British imperialism came to a focus in Joseph Chamberlain, the mouthpiece of British democracy, who assumed office as Colonial Secretary in the Salisbury Government in 1895. . . .

The man and the time arrived in 1895. As the leading British democrat and imperialist and an able public orator, parliamentary debater, and committee man, Chamberlain was one of the most influential figures in Britain. Apprehensive of Britain's position he sought as Colonial Secretary to augment British power, not by laissez-faire drift, but by government action. He offered economic assistance to the colonies, encouraged welfare in neglected colonial areas, and sought to transform "into practical results" the sentiment of imperial unity which the

Venezuela affair and the Kaiser's telegram to Kruger had evoked within the colonies. Threats to the British Empire were threats to Canada's existence. Canada therefore responded loyally and enthusiastically to Chamberlain's and the Salisbury Government's interest in and support of Canada. But Canada could not expect favours without having its own professions of loyalty and support for the Empire taken at their face value. . . .

The status of Canada was for a long time to remain a major preoccupation of many Canadians. . . . Canada was more than the colony that Britain and the United States considered it to be; rather it was on the way to becoming a colonial nation, a junior partner in the British Empire. But when Canadian leaders took advantage of Canada's colonial status to obtain benefits for Canada they showed that they were not ready to accept full national status. For example, in 1892 George E. Foster opposed the acquisition of treaty-making power by Canada on the ground that under existing conditions Canada enjoyed the advantage of British prestige and diplomatic facilities. So long as the British Empire was "bound together . . . there must be . . . one seat of sovereign and absolute power, and that seat must be . . . in the Mother-land." Again, by emphasizing the diplomatic unity of the British Empire at the conference of 1894, Foster tried to demonstrate that inter-imperial trade was a purely domestic matter. It seems certain that his purpose was to avoid an excuse for American retaliation if preferences were introduced. Similarly, as we shall see, the Laurier Government accepted a colonial status if such appeared to be of advantage to itself or to Canada. This did not mean that either Conservative or Liberal governments envisaged permanent colonial status for the country. Rather they were aware that Canada's mere existence next to an expansionist United States depended on Britain's support. As Sir Oliver Mowat, long-time Liberal Premier of Ontario, stated in an open letter in 1891 to Alexander Mackenzie, former Premier of Canada: the British connection was the greatest single source of unity to Canada.

Imperial unity, however described, was a matter of national survival for Canadians; neither Britain nor the other self-governing colonies had such a corresponding need. Canadian supporters of imperial unity were ardent Canadian nationalists, who had no intention of bartering away hard-won rights of responsible government. To them "Imperial federation," which was used indistinguishably from "Imperial unity," meant the orientation of Canadian policy towards Britain for the attainment of specific political and economic purposes. The desired end was the strengthening of Canada, not to aid Britain, but the better to defend the Dominion against the United States.

D. G. Creighton, "Sir John A. Macdonald," *Our Living Tradition Seven Canadians,* ed., Claude T. Bissell (Toronto, Published in association with Carleton University by University of Toronto Press, 1957), pp. 57-62. Reprinted by permission of the University of Toronto Press.

The Lost World of

Sir John A. Macdonald

Our interest in Macdonald is an indication of the urgency of our position. And our sense of that urgency grows in part out of an obscure, uneasy realization that we have lost or thrown away for nothing some of the valuable assets which he possessed. We are at once weaker and stronger that he was: stronger largely because we are the heirs of the good fortune which resulted from his imagination and daring; weaker because we have lost either the will or the power to use certain policies which he considered essential for the safety of our inheritance. A dim unhappy awareness of our predicament has been slowly growing in us during the last few years. What, we ask ourselves miserably, can have happened? We were all taught—it was the basic doctrine of the Liberal interpretation—that national progress was to be identified solely with emancipation from British control. We all believed that once the great crusade against British imperialism was won, we would ascend unimpeded to the serene and spacious uplands of nationhood. It

has not worked out quite that way. The uplands of nationhood have turned out to be, not serene and spacious, but troubled and restricted. And a whole generation of Canadians has been reaching the angry conclusion that it has been deceived.

Macdonald was not deceived. He realized that the nation which he hoped to create, strong and united both economically and politically, had a double task to perform. There were two goals of nationhood, not one. Canada must, in the first place, maintain a separate political existence on the North American continent; and in the second, she must achieve autonomy inside the British Empire-Commonwealth. Obviously the first national objective was the more basic and therefore the more important. It was also the more difficult to achieve; for the North American continent was dominated by the United States and, of the two imperialisms, American and British, the former was by far the more dangerous. It was upon these broad considerations that Macdonald based his foreign policy. A rough balance of power within the English-speaking world seemed essential to him to ensure Canada's survival. The diplomatic and military support of Great Britain could alone offset the political preponderance of the United States; and Macdonald proposed therefore to bring in the old world to redress the balance of the new. The Anglo-Canadian entente became the foundation of his foreign policy.

It goes without saying that, in the authorized version of Canadian history, this policy has been consistently misinterpreted. Macdonald has usually been called "an imperialist"; his party has been described as "the party of fervent imperial loyalty." These words and phrases mean, of course, exactly nothing; they are simply the Canadian equivalent of modern Com-

munist abuse. Macdonald's whole plan for Canada was essentially nationalist; every policy, political or economic, was conceived as a means to the same great nationalist goal. At Halifax, at a dinner held in September 1864, just after the Charlottetown Conference, he spoke of "founding a great British Monarchy" in North America. He tried, in the first Canadian draft of the British North America Act, to name the country he was creating "the Kingdom of Canada." And in later years he repeatedly referred to the Dominion, in language which was unusual for the time, as a separate, "auxiliary" kingdom. His view of the Empire-Commonwealth was instinctively the pluralistic view to which we have become accustomed in modern times. He was convinced, long before Confederation was achieved, that the relationship of Great Britain and Canada was rapidly changing in character. In the past it had been a connection of subordination and dependence. It was becoming an association of equals or near equals. It would be, in his own words, "a healthy and cordial alliance."

It is this word "alliance" which is the key to Macdonald's conception of the Commonwealth relationship. He hoped and believed, with all his heart, that Canada would forever remain a kingdom under the British Crown; but for him the vital reality underlying the formal association of the Empire-Commonwealth was the Anglo-Canadian entente. The word "alliance" was frequently on his lips. He took its terms very seriously. He believed that it should be expressed in fairly definite agreements between the two governments. In 1865, just before Confederation, when the question of British North American defence was up for discussion in England, and again in 1871,

when the imperial garrisons were recalled from central Canada, Macdonald obtained pledges from the British government promising military assistance to the limit in support of Canada in the event of a war with the United States. Afterwards he always referred proudly to these agreements as "treaties"; and there is no doubt he believed that similar arrangements or "treaties" must regulate any contribution that Canada might make in the future to the defence of British interests overseas. Such a contribution, of course, was never made during his lifetime. He was convinced that, while the Dominion was in the formative stages of development, the whole force of the Anglo-Canadian entente must be placed in support of Canada's weak position in North America.

It was not until the twentieth century, when his design for a transcontinental Dominion had become a reality, that his successor, Sir Robert Borden, felt strong enough to extend the operation of the alliance to Europe. Borden held fast to Macdonald's conception of the entente. He offered contributions to Great Britain's European defences in return for a voice in the determination of Commonwealth foreign policy. And the place which he secured in the Imperial War Cabinet and in the British Empire delegation to the Peace Conference gave Canada an authority and an influence in world affairs which was commensurate with the sacrifices she had made in the First World War. The ambit of the alliance had been enormously enlarged; but it had been kept true to the principles that Macdonald had laid down. It was an alliance of kingdoms, formally expressed in agreements and institutions, with benefits on each side, and shared responsibility and power. It had begun as an alliance for the defence of Canada in North America. It had become an

alliance for the assertion and protection of Canadian interests in the world at large.

In the brief space of a quarter-century, this alliance, in both its European and its North American aspects, was abandoned by Mackenzie King. King could hardly have chosen a more inappropriate moment in which to let it go. The first half of the twentieth century witnessed a persistent decline in the power of Great Britain. It saw an even more impressive and steady rise in the preponderating authority of the United States. The imbalance of power in the English-speaking world, the overwhelming influence of the United States in the Americas, grew increasingly obvious; but King, with an old man's obsession with the now antiquated and meaningless cause of autonomy inside the British Empire, chose this particular time to cut us off from necessary associations with Great Britain and to plunge us deeper and deeper into continental commitments with the United States. If he had wished to do so, he might in 1939 have forced the creation of a Commonwealth Council which would have given Canada a voice in the conduct of the war in Europe and support in defence arrangements with the United States in North America. He repudiated the very idea of such a body. With his mind in the past, he regarded any formal association with Great Britain as "imperial centralization." He preferred to let the United States and Great Britain run the war in Europe. He preferred to do his own negotiating in North America. And whereas Macdonald negotiated from positions of relative strength, King negotiated from positions of serious weakness, and—we are told by those who ought to know best —in a spirit of ready compliance. The result has been the series of discreet, informal bargains with the United States

which, since 1940, has been one of the most distinctive features of Canadian foreign policy.

It is this which has filled the Canadian people with misgiving and apprehension. It is this which has awakened a new interest in Macdonald and his national Canadian design. Macdonald's prime purpose was to found a transcontinental nation which would have a separate and autonomous existence in North America. His fundamental aim was to protect Canada from the dangers of continentalism; and it is the dangers of continentalism, economic, political, military, which now seem to be pressing in upon us steadily and from every side. We are worried today, as we never were before, about the ownership of our strategic raw materials, our metals, our new sources of fuel and power. We have a resentful feeling that we are overpersuaded into an unwelcome arrangement about the St. Lawrence Seaway, which we are now trying to rectify by additional expenditures of our own; and we have an uneasy suspicion that the unpublicized negotiations which are going forward about the Columbia River will end in some serious reduction or abandonment of our unquestionable rights. Under persuasion which may very well be heavy pressure, are we being fitted smoothly and permanently into a continental capitalist organization, a continental power grid, a continental defence system? In Europe, NATO is a collective defensive enterprise; but in North America it is a two-power organization in which Canada can accept only the assistance, and the direction, of the United States. In the north, Americans build and man our radar installations; and in the east, in Newfoundland and Labrador, they hold and occupy military bases. The foreigner sits firmly astride the eastern approaches to

our country; and the base, a primitive form of military imperialism, grimly questions Canada's claim to control her own destiny.

It is this sense of the danger overshadowing the main purpose of our existence which has brought Canadians back with interest and with almost the excitement of rediscovery to Sir John Macdonald.

Suggested Reading

L'Action Nationale, *La pensée de Henri Bourassa*, (Montreal, 1954).

C. Berger, *The Sense of Power Studies in the Ideas of Canadian Imperialism, 1867-1914*, (Toronto, 1970).

————, ed., *Imperial Relations in the Age of Laurier*, (Toronto, Canadian Historical Readings, 1969).

C. A. Bodelsen, *Studies in Mid-Victorian Imperialism*, (London, reprint 1960).

R. C. Brown, *Canadian National Policy 1883-1900 A Study in Canadian-American Relations*, (Princeton, 1964).

H. Borden, ed., *Sir Robert Laird Borden: His Memoirs*, (Toronto, 1938).

G. R. Cook, *The Politics of John W. Dafoe and the Free Press*, (Toronto, 1963).

D. G. Creighton, *John A. Macdonald The Old Chieftain*, (Toronto, 1955).

J. Dafoe, *Laurier A Study in Canadian Politics*, (Toronto, 1922).

G. T. Denison, *The Struggle for Imperial Unity*, (Toronto, 1909).

W. S. Evans, *The Canadian Contingents and Canadian Imperialism*, (London, 1901).

R. Faber, *The Vision and the Need Late Victorian Imperialist Aims*, (London, 1966).

D. K. Fieldhouse, " 'Imperialism': An Historiographical Revision," *Economic History Review*, Second Series, Vol. XIV (no. 2, 1961), pp. 187-209.

W. L. Grant and F. Hamilton, *Principal Grant*, (Toronto, 1904).

D. C. Gordon, *The Dominion Partnership in Imperial Defense, 1870-1914*, (Toronto, 1967).

J. Hobson, *Imperialism A Study*, (London, 1902).

J. E. Kendle, *The Colonial and Imperial Conferences 1887-1911 A Study in Imperial Organization*, (London, 1967).

W. L. Langer, "A Critique of Imperialism," *Foreign Affairs*, Vol. XIV (Oct. 1935), pp. 102-114.

A. R. M. Lower, *Canada Nation and Neighbour*, (Toronto, 1952).

A. Macphail, *Essays in Politics*, (London, 1909).

C. Murrow, *Henri Bourassa and French-Canadian Nationalism Opposition to Empire*, (Montreal, 1968).

M. P. O'Connell, "The Ideas of Henri Bourassa," *Canadian Journal of Economics and Political Science*, Vol. XIX (Aug., 1953), pp. 361-76.

N. Penlington, *Canada and Imperialism 1896-1899*, (Toronto, 1965).

R. A. Preston, *Canada and "Imperial Defense" A Study in the Origins of the British Commonwealth's Defense Organization, 1867-1919*, (Toronto, 1967).

A. Siegfried, *The Race Question in Canada*, (Toronto, Carleton Library, 1966).

O. D. Skelton, *Life and Letters of Sir Wilfrid Laurier*, (Toronto, 1921).

G. Smith, *In the Court of History An Apology for those Canadians who were opposed to the South African War*, (Toronto, 1902).

E. Stokes, *The Political Ideas of English Imperialism An Inaugural Lecture Given in the University College of Rhodesia and Nyasaland*, (London, 1960).

A. P. Thornton, *The Imperial Idea and its Enemies,* (London, 1959).

———, *Doctrines of Imperialism,* (New York, 1965).

J. E. Tyler, *The Struggle for Imperial Unity 1868-95,* (London, 1938).

F. H. Underhill, *In Search of Canadian Liberalism,* (Toronto, 1960).

M. Wade, *The French Canadians 1760-1945,* (Toronto, 1955).

———, "Olivar Asselin," in *Canada's Past and Present: A Dialogue,* ed., R. L. McDougall, (Toronto, 1965), pp. 134-57.

E. Wallace, *Goldwin Smith Victorian Liberal,* (Toronto, 1957).

W. S. Wallace, *The Growth of Canadian National Feeling,* (Toronto, 1927).

J. S. Willison, *Sir George Parkin A Biography,* (London, 1929).

H. A. Wilson, *The Imperial Policy of Sir Robert Borden,* (Gainsville, Florida, 1966).

S. F. Wise and R. C. Brown, *Canada Views the United States Nineteenth Century Political Attitudes,* (Toronto, 1967).

Date Due

4 5 6 7 — 76 75

ISSUES IN CANADIAN HISTORY

General Editor
J. L. GRANATSTEIN

Imperialism and
Nationalism,
1884-1914:
A Conflict in
Canadian Thought